From Your Friends At **The MAILBOX®**

OCTOBER

A MONTH OF REPRODUCIBLES AT YOUR FINGERTIPS!

Grade 1

Editor:
Susan Hohbach Walker

Writers:
Catherine Broome, Lisa Buchholz, Amy Erickson,
Amy Harders, Lucia Kemp Henry,
Cynthia Holcomb, Sharon Murphy

Art Coordinator:
Clevell Harris

Artists:
Nick Greenwood, Clevell Harris, Sheila Krill,
Rob Mayworth, Kimberly Richard,
Rebecca Saunders, Barry Slate, Donna K. Teal

Cover Artist:
Jennifer Tipton Bennett

©1999 by THE EDUCATION CENTER, INC.
All rights reserved.
ISBN #1-56234-261-4

Except as provided for herein, no part of this publication may be reproduced or transmitted in any form or by any means, electronic or mechanical, including photocopying, recording, or storing in any information storage and retrieval system or electronic on-line bulletin board, without prior written permission from The Education Center, Inc. Permission is given to the original purchaser to reproduce patterns and reproducibles for individual classroom use only and not for resale or distribution. Reproduction for an entire school or school system is prohibited. Please direct written inquiries to The Education Center, Inc., P.O. Box 9753, Greensboro, NC 27429-0753. The Education Center®, *The Mailbox*®, and the mailbox/post/grass logo are registered trademarks of The Education Center, Inc. All other brand or product names are trademarks or registered trademarks of their respective companies.

Manufactured in the United States
10 9 8 7 6 5 4 3 2 1

Table Of Contents

October Calendar Capers 3
Daily activities to help you celebrate events in October.

Events And Activities For The Family 4
Three events and activities for families and students to explore at home.

Harvest Happenings 5
These ideas for celebrating fall are the pick of the crop!

Oktoberfest 11
Add a taste of Germany to your lesson plans with this selection of reproducibles.

Fire Prevention Week 17
Use the activities in this unit to teach your students the importance of fire safety.

National Metric Week 21
You'll have ten times the fun as you celebrate the importance of the metric system.

Columbus Day 25
Discover the importance of Columbus's journey by using these fascinating activities and reproducibles.

Happy Birthday, Steven Kellogg! 29
Celebrate the birthday of this famous children's artist and storyteller with the help of these activities.

Spiders 33
Spin a web of knowledge about spiders with these amazing arachnid activities.

Happy Halloween! 37
Spooky, creepy, and just plain fun are the types of activities that will haunt you as you complete this Halloween unit.

National Pizza Month 43
This saucy unit will treat your students to a big slice of basic skills practice.

National Popcorn Poppin' Month 49
Pique students' interest about popcorn with this sizzling series of ideas.

National Cookie Month 55
Your little cookie crunchers will be eager to take a bite out of learning using this tasty theme.

Computer Learning Month 59
Use this set of reproducibles to emphasize the importance of computers and other technology in your classroom.

Answer Keys 64

Name _____

October Calendar

October Calendar Capers

Monday	Tuesday	Wednesday	Thursday	Friday
October is National Dessert Month. Invite students to sample bite-size pieces of eclairs, strudels, tarts, cream puffs, or other tasty treats. 	On October 2, 1950, the PEANUTS® comic strip, featuring Charlie Brown® and Snoopy®, was first published. Share some of these popular comic strips with your students. 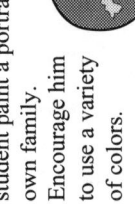	October 4 is Ten-Four Day. Explain to students that radio operators use the code words "ten-four" for "yes." Encourage students to use this special code when giving affirmative replies today. 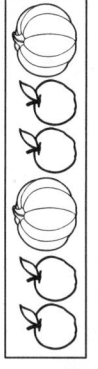	October is National Pasta Month. Give each youngster an assortment of uncooked pasta. Have him sort, count, and then graph the number of each type of pasta.  	The first week in October is Get Organized Week. Ask students to organize their desks, backpacks, and notebooks. 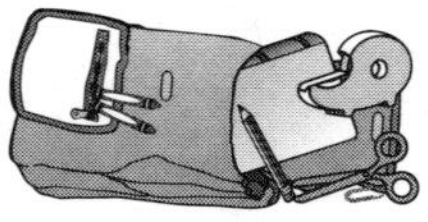
Have each youngster draw a picture of a happy scarecrow covered with friendly crows.  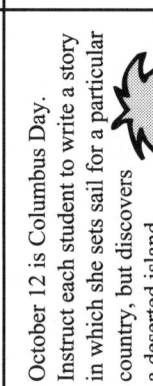	October is National Clock Month. Ask students to brainstorm problems that would arise if we did not have clocks.  	Have each youngster collect a variety of leaves and trace them on a sheet of paper. Then instruct him to color the resulting leaf shapes. 	October 12 is Columbus Day. Instruct each student to write a story in which she sets sail for a particular country, but discovers a deserted island instead.	Direct each student to create a pattern by drawing fall objects. Then have each youngster challenge a classmate to predict what the next object in his pattern will be.
Squirrels store nuts for winter at this time of year. Ask students to name things that people store.  	October 15 is National Grouch Day. Read aloud *Alexander And The Terrible, Horrible, No Good, Very Bad Day* by Judith Viorst (Aladdin Paperbacks, 1987).  	October 16, the birthdate of Noah Webster, is Dictionary Day. Webster is well known for compiling *Webster's Dictionary*. Provide each youngster with a list of five words and have her look them up in a dictionary. 	The third full week in October is National School Bus Safety Week. Review bus safety rules. Then direct small groups of students to make posters that promote bus safety. 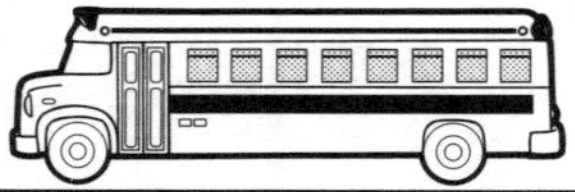	Artist Pablo Picasso was born on October 25, 1881. Have each student paint a portrait of his own family. Encourage him to use a variety of colors.
Ask each student to write a math story problem about squirrels and nuts.  	Take students outside and have each of them hold a sheet of paper on a tree trunk. Instruct each youngster to rub a crayon on her paper to reveal the bark's texture.  	Challenge students to make a list of the many things that can be done with a pumpkin. 	The Statue of Liberty was dedicated on October 28, 1886. Have youngsters work in small groups to sculpt clay models of the statue.	October 31 is National Magic Day. Perform a magic trick for your students. 

©1999 The Education Center, Inc. • *October Monthly Reproducibles* • Grade 1 • TEC960

Note To The Teacher: Highlight special days and events with these fact-filled ideas.

Name _____

October Events
Family activities

October
Events And Activities For The Family

Directions: Select at least one activity below to complete as a family by the end of October.
(Challenge: See if your family can complete all three activities.)

On A Roll

Count on this "die-namite" game to boost math skills! Two or more players and at least one die are required. To play a round, each player, in turn, rolls a die. The player who rolls the highest number earns one point. Players roll again in the event of a tie. Play continues in a similar manner until one player accumulates a predetermined number of points. Vary this game to reinforce addition skills by having each player roll a pair of dice. The player with the greatest sum for each round earns a point.

National Clock Month

In no time at all, your child will be a time-telling pro with this nifty clock project! To make a clock, first mark the center of a large paper plate. Then, with a pencil, lightly mark the plate to indicate the appropriate position for each numeral, or make the numerals with dotted lines. Have your child write or trace the numerals. Then help your youngster measure and cut out one 3 3/4" x 3/4" and one 3" x 3/4" piece of construction paper. Have him or her cut a point at one end of each piece. Then, with a brass fastener, carefully attach the resulting clock hands to the center of the plate as shown. Throughout your daily schedule this month, invite your youngster to move the clock hands to show important times, such as dinnertime, TV time, and even bedtime! Now that's a timely teaching tool!

National Dessert Month

This appetizing idea is served with a heaping cup of reading and a pinch of math. Cook up this recipe with your child in honor of National Dessert Month. Bon appétit!

Perfect Pudding Parfaits (Serves approximately 4)
You Need:
1 small package instant pudding in the flavor of your choice
2 cups milk
1 small container of frozen whipped topping, thawed
chopped nuts or chocolate sprinkles (optional)
1 parfait glass or dessert dish for each serving

Directions:
1. Pour the pudding mix into a small bowl.
2. Add milk.
3. Beat until thick.
4. Place 2–3 spoonfuls of pudding in each parfait glass or dessert dish.
5. Place 2–3 spoonfuls of whipped topping atop the pudding.
6. Continue alternating the remaining pudding and topping in a like manner.
7. If desired, add nuts or sprinkles to the top of each dessert.

Variations: Layer fruit, marshmallows, chocolate syrup, or candy-bar pieces with pudding and whipped topping.

©1999 The Education Center, Inc. • *October Monthly Reproducibles* • Grade 1 • TEC960

Note To The Teacher: Distribute one copy of this reproducible to each student at the beginning of the month. Encourage each family to complete at least one activity by the end of October.

HARVEST HAPPENINGS

These autumn activities are the cream of the crop! They are just "ripe" for young learners and are guaranteed to harvest bushels of fun!

A harvest moon is the very bright full moon that occurs near September 22 or 23.

Corn plants range in height from approximately 3 feet to 20 feet.

Most pumpkins weigh about 15–30 pounds, but some weigh as much as 800 pounds.

A typical grocery store sells more than 1,000 foods that are made with corn or corn products.

A Bushel Of Math

Watch computation skills grow with this seasonal workmat activity! Give each student a copy of page 10 and have him color his basket and vegetables. Then direct him to cut along the dotted lines to create vegetable cards. Explain to youngsters that they will use these cards to tell a story. Tell a simple story, such as the one shown, and have each student manipulate his vegetable cards to correspond with it. With students' help, write a number sentence on the chalkboard to match the story. Provide addition and subtraction practice with similar stories involving these picture cards. Then have youngsters make their own stories with their cards and workmats. Invite several youngsters to share their stories with the class. Next ask each student to glue his vegetable cards on his workmat to represent his favorite story. Then have him write a number sentence to describe it on the center band of his basket.

Pick A Pair

Count on this memory game to reap grade-A number-word skills! Duplicate a copy of page 8 on white construction paper and a copy of page 9 on yellow construction paper for each student. Have each youngster cut along the solid grid lines on both pages to create game cards. Provide each student with a storage envelope for her cards if desired. To play, have each youngster name and count the pictures on each white card (from page 8); then have her pair it with a yellow card (from page 9) to show the corresponding number word. Or have a pair of students place one set of white and yellow cards facedown on a tabletop. The students then take turns flipping over two cards (one of each color) in an attempt to find matching pairs. If a match is made, the student keeps the pair of cards. If no match is made, she turns the cards facedown again. The student with the most cards at the end of the game is the winner. Now that's a memorable way to reinforce number words!

Farmer Frank picked three pumpkins. Farmer Fran picked five ears of corn. How many vegetables did they pick in all?

Name _____

Cut and glue to match.

Clever Crows

Harvest Happenings
Initial consonants: *b, f, m, s, t*

Bonus Box: *Bird* begins with *b*. On the back of this sheet, draw things that begin with *b*.

©1999 The Education Center, Inc. • *October Monthly Reproducibles* • Grade 1 • TEC960

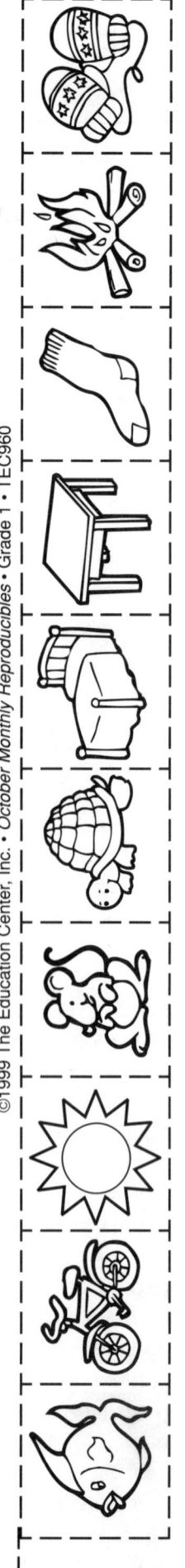

Name _____

Harvest Happenings
Initial consonants: c, d, l, p, r

What's In The Pumpkin Patch?

Write the letter that begins each picture name.

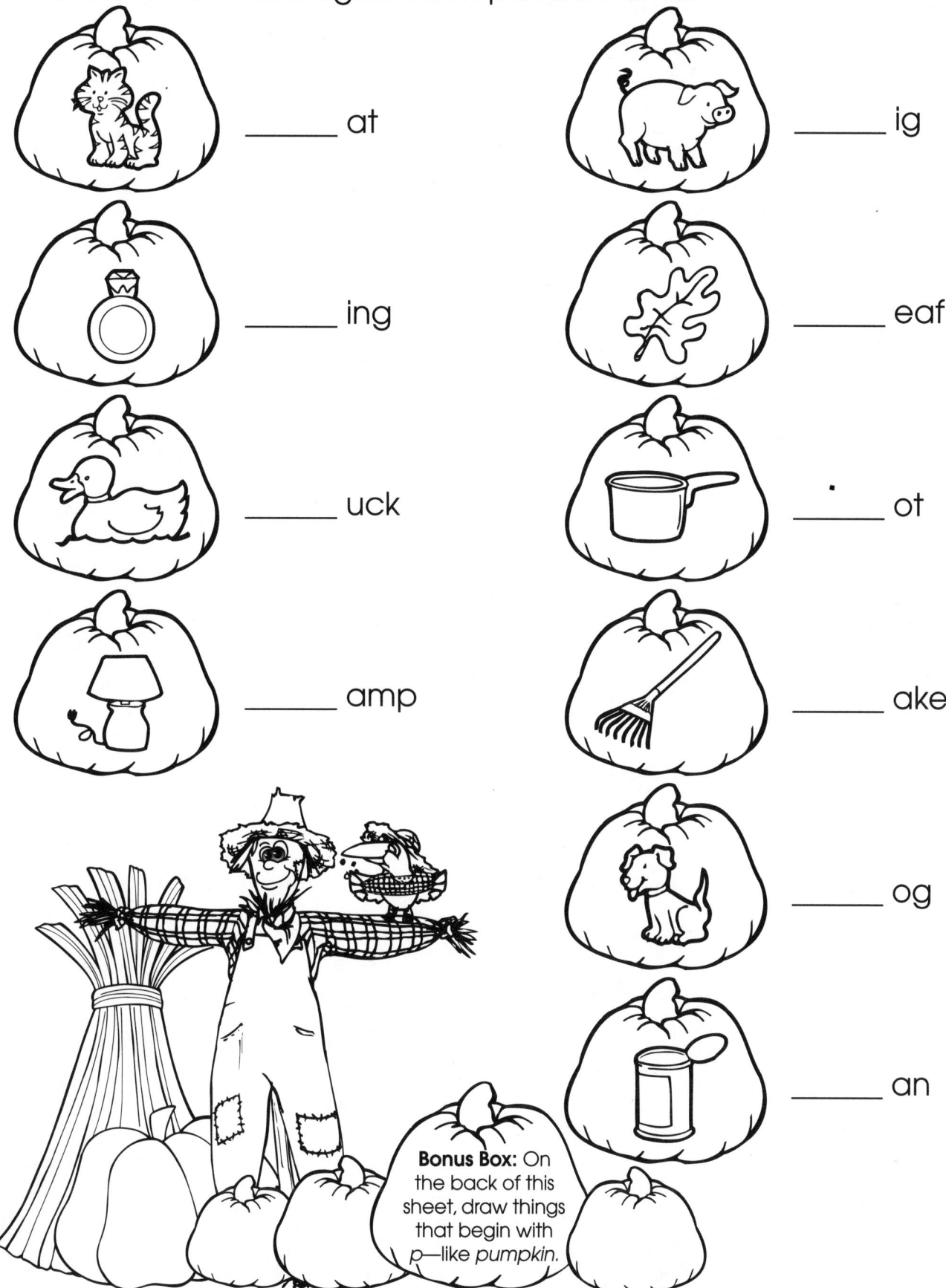

____ at

____ ing

____ uck

____ amp

____ ig

____ eaf

____ ot

____ ake

____ og

____ an

Bonus Box: On the back of this sheet, draw things that begin with p—like pumpkin.

©1999 The Education Center, Inc. • October Monthly Reproducibles • Grade 1 • TEC960

7

Harvest Happenings
Number words/picture cards

Pick A Pair

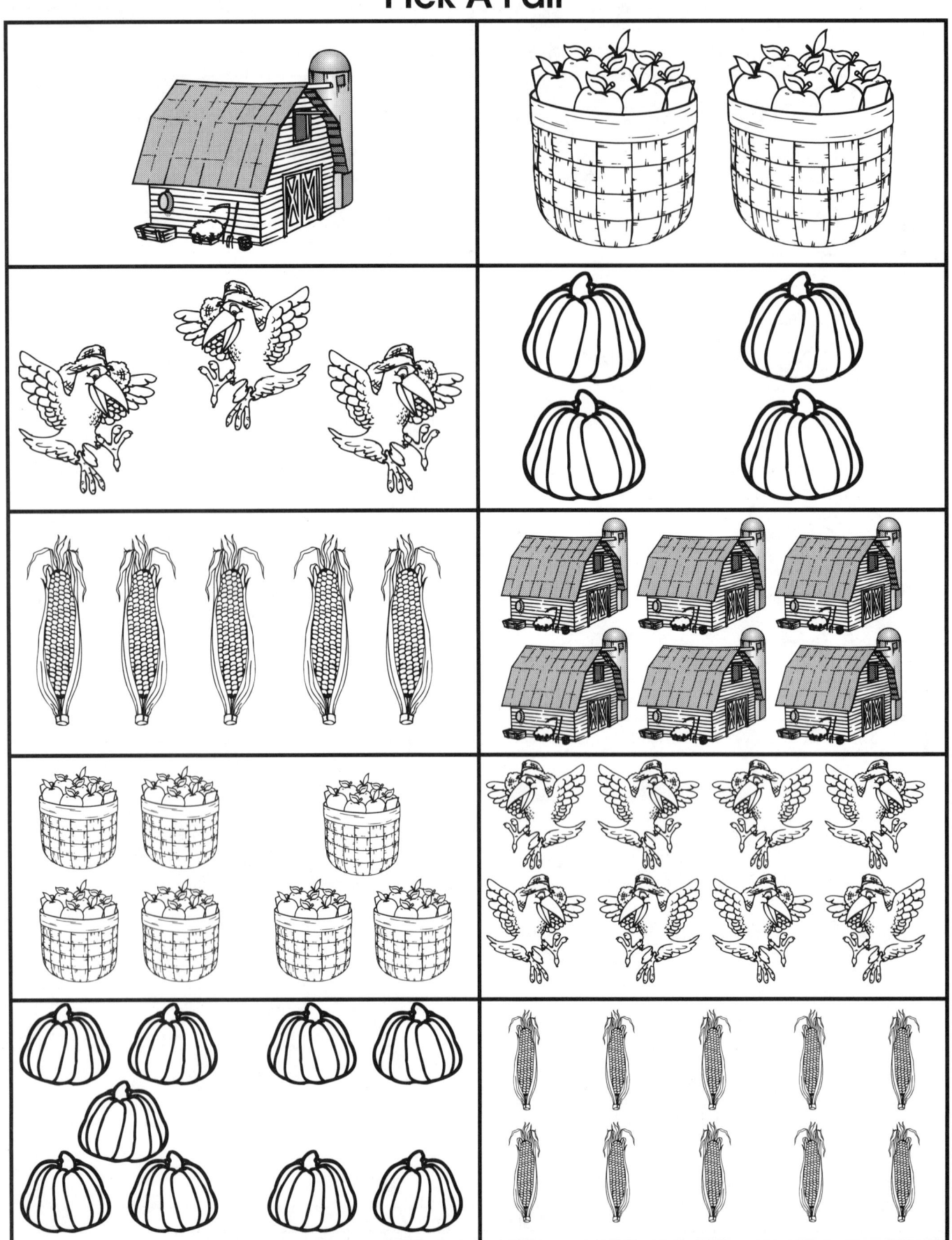

©1999 The Education Center, Inc. • *October Monthly Reproducibles* • Grade 1 • TEC960

Note To The Teacher: Use with "Pick A Pair" on page 5.

Harvest Happenings
Number words/word cards

Pick A Pair

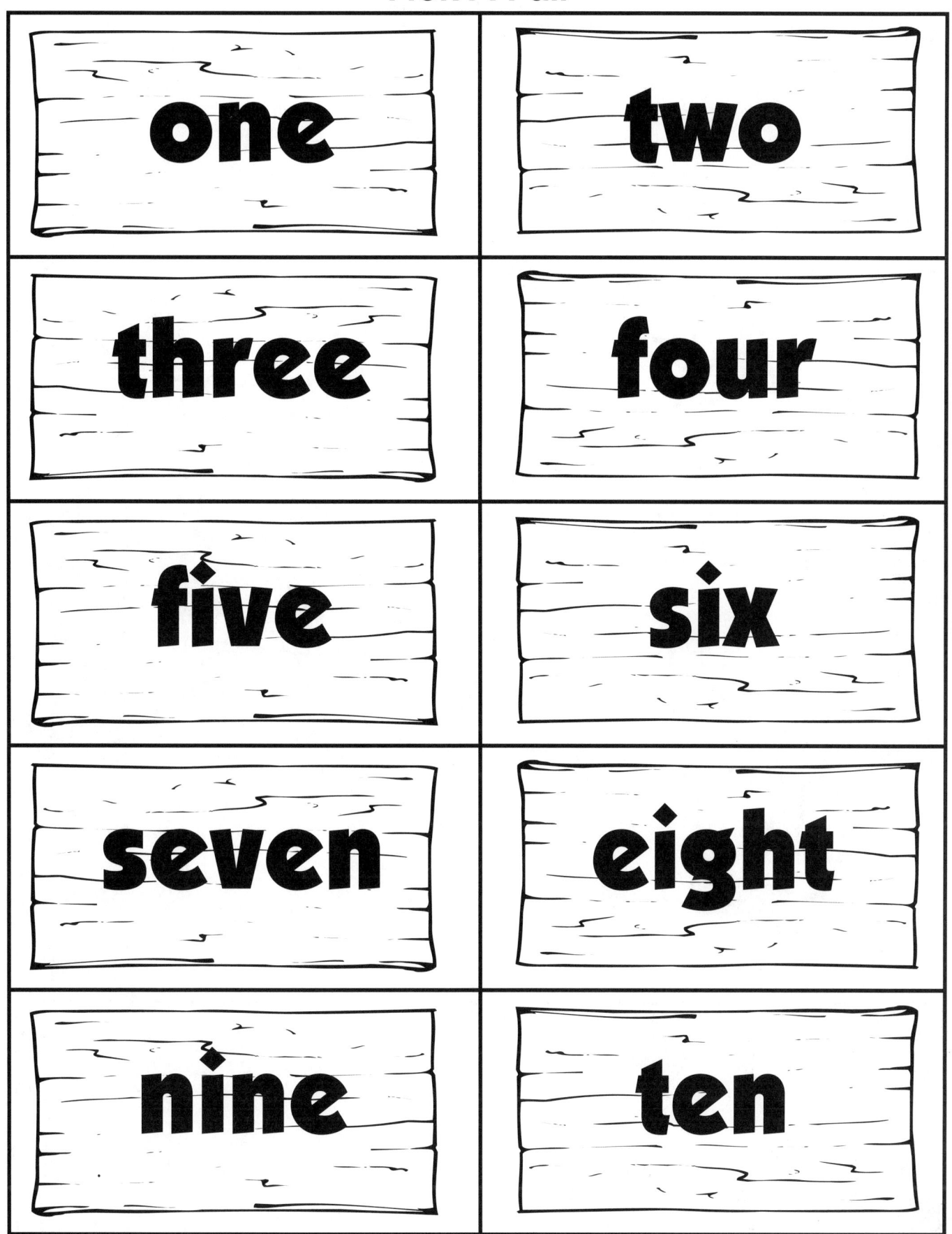

©1999 The Education Center, Inc. • October Monthly Reproducibles • Grade 1 • TEC960

Note To The Teacher: Use with "Pick A Pair" on page 5.

9

Name _____

Harvest Happenings
Math workmat

A Bushel Of Math

Follow your teacher's directions.

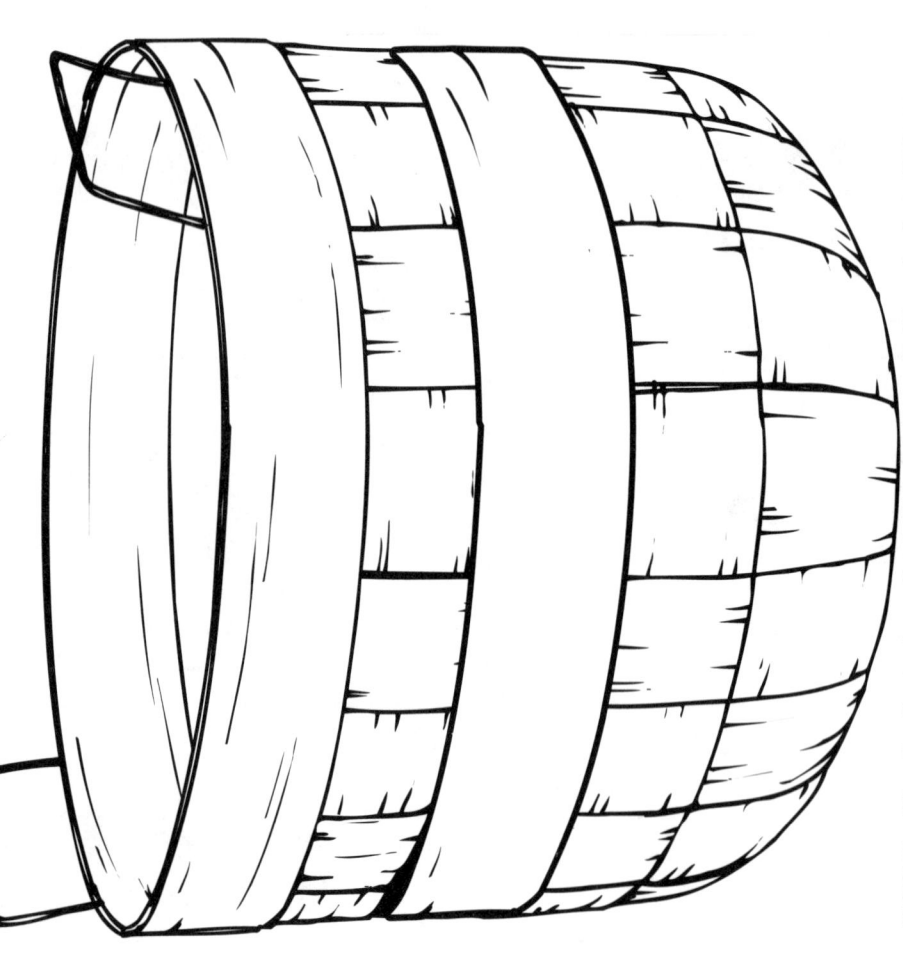

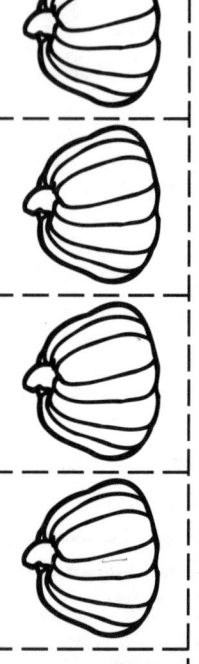

Note To The Teacher: Use with "A Bushel Of Math" on page 5.

©1999 The Education Center, Inc. • *October Monthly Reproducibles* • Grade 1 • TEC960

Oktoberfest

Fill your classroom with fall festivities by saluting a well-known seasonal German celebration called Oktoberfest. The festival, held in Munich, Germany, each year lasts for 16 days and is filled with wonderful German folk customs, music, and food.

A Journey Through Germany

The countryside of Germany is known for its quaint villages, beautiful castles, majestic mountains, and fairy-tale forests. Take your youngsters on an imaginary trip to these classic German sights via the map on page 15. Give a copy of "Hamburg Hike" to each child; then have her take out a black crayon. Explain to your youngsters that they will be drawing the route that Bader Bear will take through the German countryside on his way to the village. Ask your youngsters to help you identify and name each site on Bader's map. Then have them listen and respond to the following directions:

1. Put your crayon on the X **near** Bader Bear. The trail will begin here. Draw a line **above** the lake to the bridge.
2. Next, continue the trail **across** the bridge.
3. Now draw the trail **up** to the old tree.
4. Continue the trail **under** the cow.
5. Then draw the trail **above** the mountain.
6. Next, draw the trail **through** the castle.
7. Finally, draw the trail **into** the village.
8. Finish the map for Bader Bear by coloring each place along the trail.

To vary this activity, label a copy of page 15 with "North," "South," "East," and "West" in the appropriate locations before duplicating a class set. Then have students respond to questions using the cardinal directions as their guide. For example you might say, "What is directly east of the bridge?"

Frankfurter Fest!

Did you know that one of children's favorite foods originated in Germany? Sausages of all kinds are a traditional German food and one particular kind of sausage, the frankfurter, originated in Frankfurt, Germany. The American version of the frankfurter is none other than—the hot dog! To find out how your youngsters like to top off this tasty German American food, distribute a copy of "Frankfurter Fest!" on page 16 to each child. Read the question aloud with your students; then review the topping choices on the list. Ask each child to color the box near his favorite topping. Next have him color the hot dog pattern at the bottom of the page, cut it out, and glue it to a six-inch paper plate. Direct each child to use one of the following art materials to top his faux frankfurter with his favorite condiment:

ketchup—red paint in a squeeze bottle
mustard—yellow paint in a squeeze bottle
chili—small dry beans mixed into brown paint
sauerkraut—thinly shredded white paper or clear plastic Easter grass

Help each youngster post his completed hot dog on a bulletin-board bar graph (similar to the graph on page 16). When this hands-on graph is completed, ask each child to transfer the data to the smaller graph on his activity page by coloring in spaces for each chosen topping. Discuss the graph with your youngsters; then have each child write the name of the topping with the most votes on the line to the left of the graph.

Name _____

Town Sounds

Color by the code.
Write.

Color Code:
h = red
j = blue
n = green
w = yellow

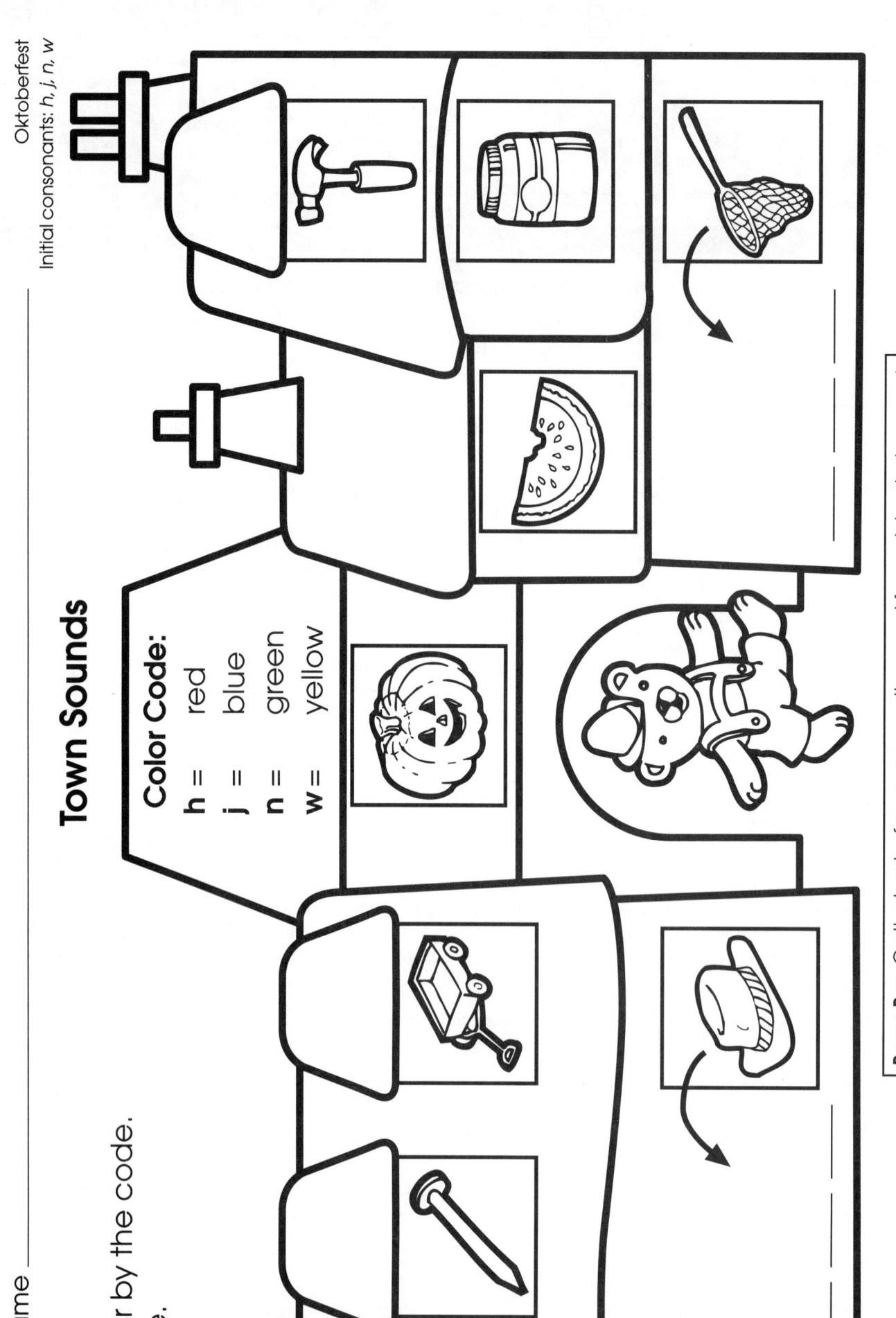

Oktoberfest
Initial consonants: h, j, n, w

Bonus Box: On the back of your paper, write a word for each beginning sound.

©1999 The Education Center, Inc. • *October Monthly Reproducibles* • Grade 1 • TEC960

Name _____

Oktoberfest
Sets to twelve

Pretzel Sets

Count. Write.

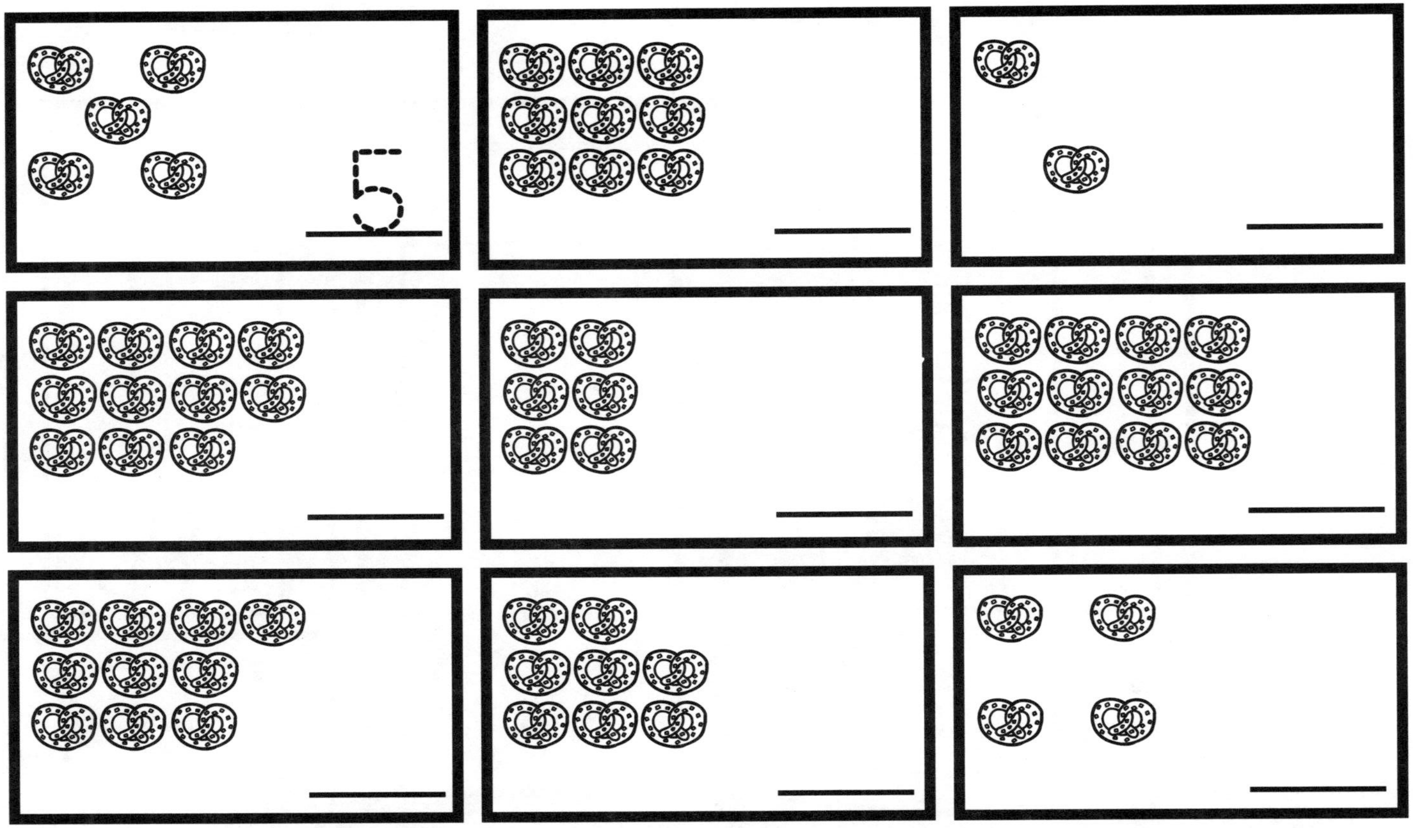

		5

Draw.

7		3

Note To The Teacher: For a follow-up activity, give each child 12 minipretzel twists. Direct him to make sets of varying amounts. After he makes each set, have him tell you the amount.

©1999 The Education Center, Inc. • *October Monthly Reproducibles* • Grade 1 • TEC960

Name _____

Oktoberfest
Rhyming words

Pairs In The Palace

Match the pictures that rhyme.
Cut. Glue. Write.

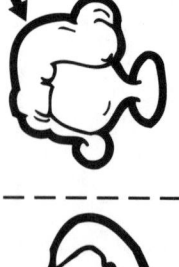

Bonus Box: On the back of this sheet, draw two more sets of rhyming pictures.

©1999 The Education Center, Inc. • October Monthly Reproducibles • Grade 1 • TEC960

Name _____

Oktoberfest
Position words

Hamburg Hike

Listen and do.

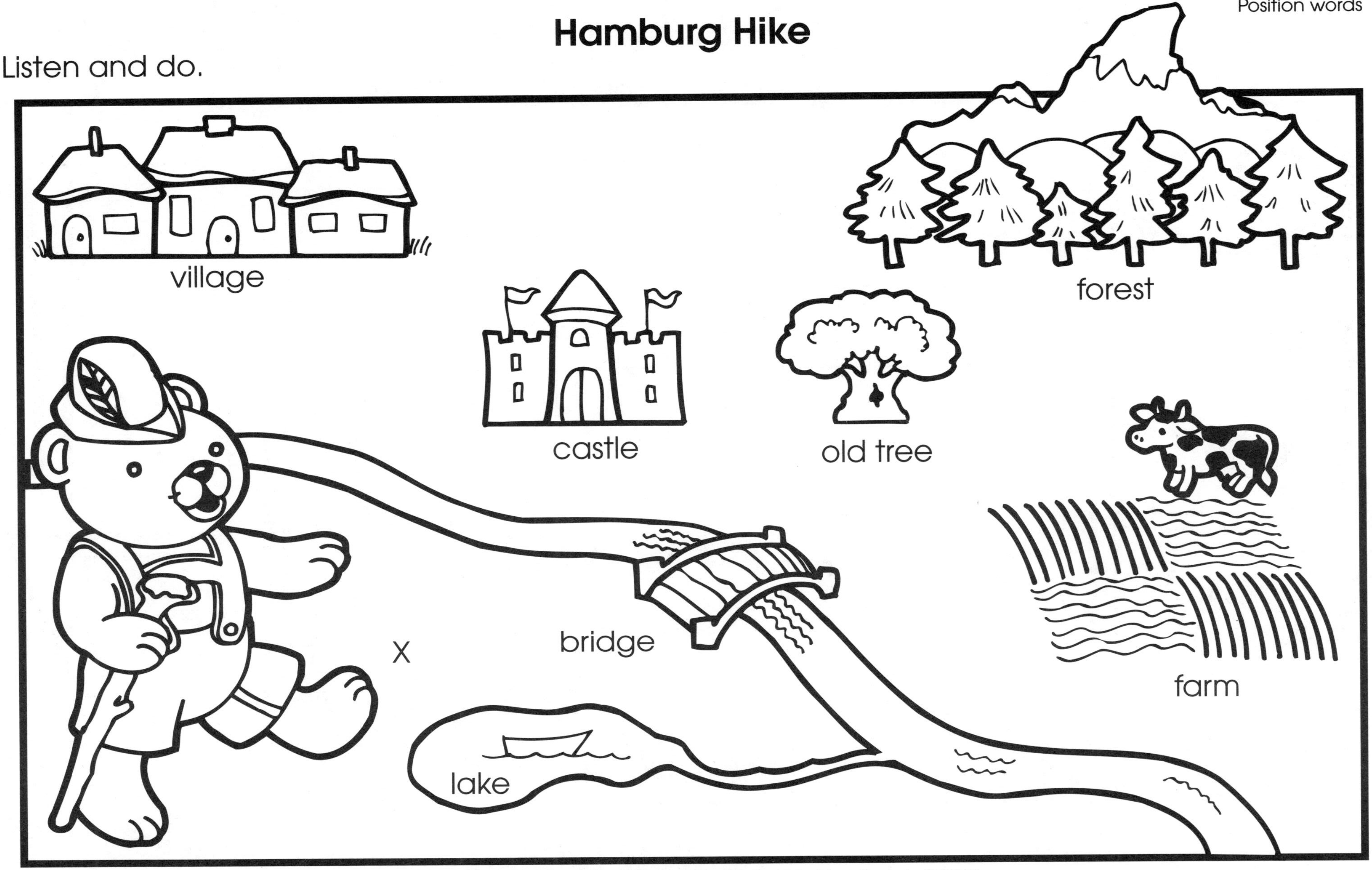

Note To The Teacher: Use with "A Journey Through Germany" on page 11.

©1999 The Education Center, Inc. • *October Monthly Reproducibles* • Grade 1 • TEC960

15

Name _____

Oktoberfest Graphing

Frankfurter Fest!

What is our favorite hot dog topping?

My favorite is

☐ ketchup
☐ mustard
☐ chili
☐ sauerkraut

The class favorite is:

_____

ketchup	mustard	chili	sauerkraut

©1999 The Education Center, Inc. • October Monthly Reproducibles • Grade 1 • TEC960

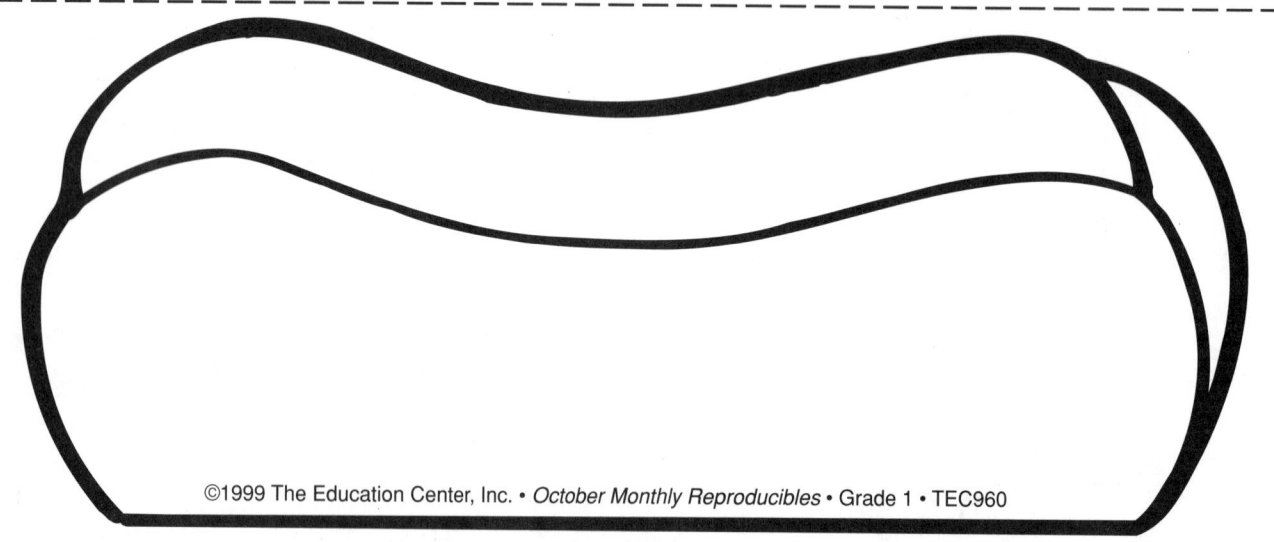

©1999 The Education Center, Inc. • October Monthly Reproducibles • Grade 1 • TEC960

16 **Note To The Teacher:** Use with "Frankfurter Fest!" on page 11.

Fire Prevention Week

Fire Prevention Week is observed annually during the week in which October 8 falls. It commemorates the Great Chicago Fire that began on that day in 1871. Prepare for the event with the following ideas that are sure to spark your students' interest in fire safety.

Fire And Flames—Friendly Or Fearsome?

With so much emphasis on preventing fires, students may forget that fire is often beneficial as long as it is used safely. Ask your students to brainstorm ways that fire can be used to help people, such as fireplaces, campfires, controlled brush burning, and trash disposal. Record their responses. Next have your students list ways that fire can be dangerous, such as forest fires, house fires, or car fires. Distribute crayons and a sheet of drawing paper to each student, and have her draw a picture showing fire being either helpful or harmful. Provide time for each child to share her completed drawing with the class. Lead the class in a discussion of the situation depicted in each illustration to reinforce the importance and the dangers of fire.

Fire-Safety Fashions

Familiarize your students with fire-safety smarts by having them wear what they learn. After a discussion on fire-safety dos and don'ts, have each child create a vest illustrated with safety tips. In advance, gather a class supply of brown paper grocery bags. To create a vest, spread out the bag on a flat surface and cut as shown. Provide crayons and markers for students to use as they decorate their vests with pictures showing fire prevention and safety rules. When the projects are completed, let your students parade around the school grounds to show off their fire-safety fashions.

Call 911!

Most students are familiar with the number to call in an emergency situation—but once they've dialed, will they know what to say? Provide the opportunity for students to role-play an emergency situation in which they must report a fire. Have an unplugged telephone handy, and have each child practice calling 911 to report a neighborhood fire. Remind students to speak plainly and give as much necessary information as possible. (After everyone has had a chance to practice, reinforce that this number should be dialed only in the event of a *real* emergency.) In case of a fire, help will be just a phone call away!

Name_____   Fire Prevention Week
Ordinal numbers

Pups In Line

Cut.
Glue to match.

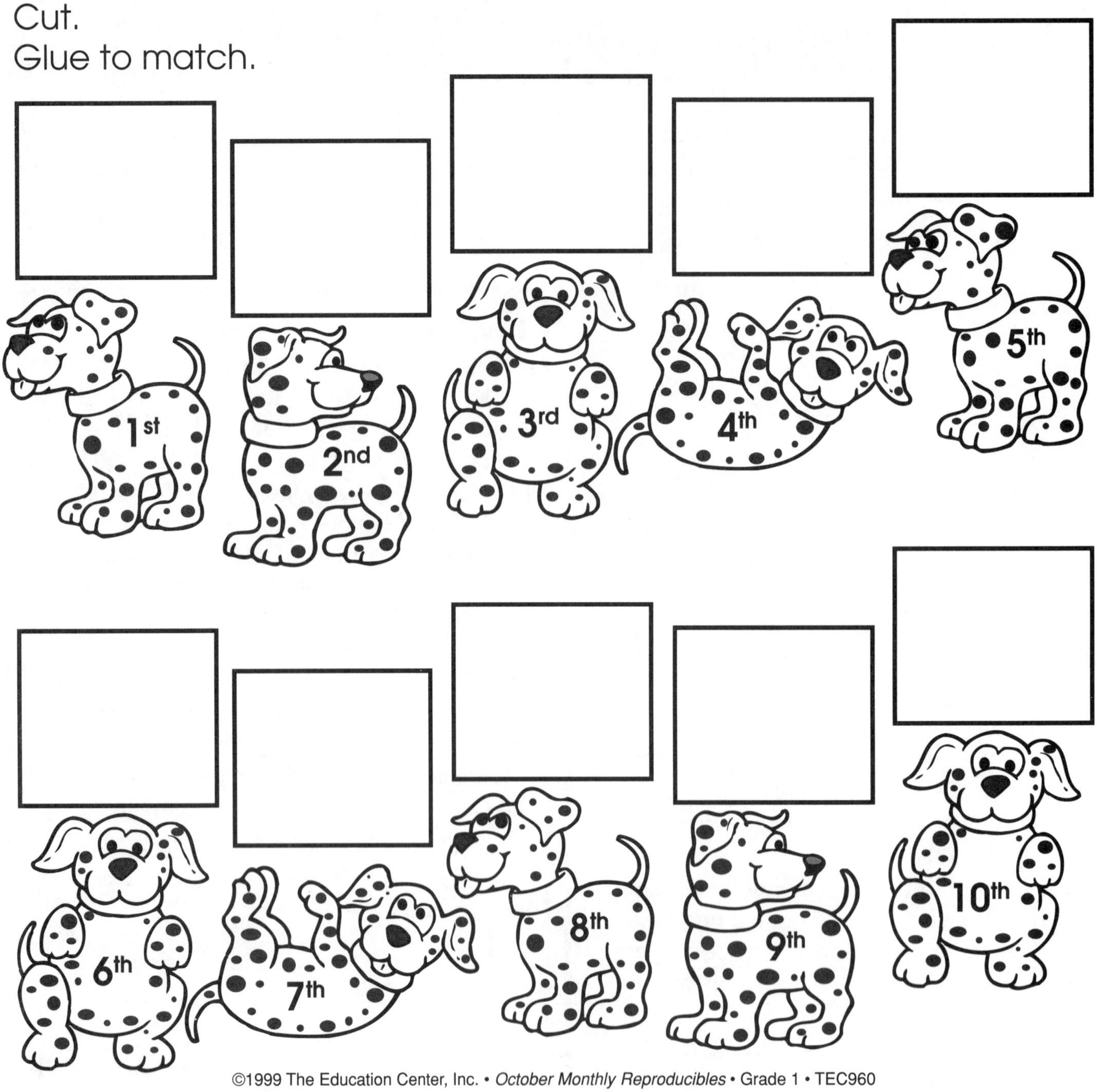

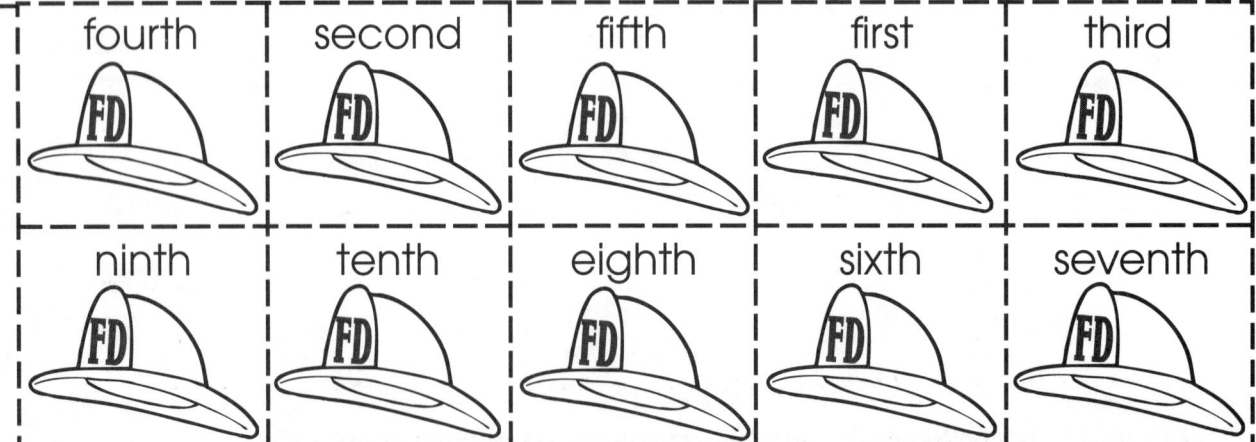

Name_____

Fire Prevention Week
Reading comprehension

Be Fire Smart!

Read.
Choose a word.
Write.

Do you know what to do if there is a fire?

1. Stay _____ the smoke.

   under
   ugly

2. Feel the _____ to see if it is hot.

   drip
   door

3. Go to a _____ place.

   safe
   sing

4. Do not go back _____ .

   idea
   inside

5. Call 911 for _____ .

   happy
   help

Write a fire safety rule.

_____

©1999 The Education Center, Inc. • October Monthly Reproducibles • Grade 1 • TEC960

Name_____ Fire Prevention Week
ABC order

Wet Words

Write each set of words in ABC order.

stop
drop
roll
crawl

smoke
fire
truck
hose

1.
2.
3.
4.

1.
2.
3.
4.

20 ©1999 The Education Center, Inc. • *October Monthly Reproducibles* • Grade 1 • TEC960

NATIONAL METRIC WEEK

Don't monkey around! It's time to get busy celebrating National Metric Week. Held in the tenth month during the week containing the tenth day, this event promotes awareness of the metric system (based on tens) and its importance to our society.

Monkey Measurement

Your students will go bananas over this "ape-pealing" measurement center! To prepare, make 10 brown construction-paper copies of the monkey pattern on page 24. Cut out the monkey patterns; then label each with a different letter from *A* to *J*. Punch a hole through the black dot on each monkey, and tie a length of yarn (up to 15 centimeters long) through the hole to create a tail. Cut each tail to a different length in centimeters. Place the monkeys in a center with a centimeter ruler, lined paper, and pencils for recording. Instruct each child to measure one monkey's tail at a time. Then ask her to record her findings for each monkey by writing its letter and its tail measurement on a sheet of paper.

Container Comparison

Have your students swing on into this hands-on exploration center. Fill a sand or water table or other large tub with sand, dry rice or beans, or water. Then place several clearly labeled one-liter, one-pint, and one-quart containers in the center. Encourage students to experiment with the amount each container will hold. Challenge students to discover which containers hold more or less, how many pints fill a liter, etc. After comparing containers, your students will have a better understanding of the volume of a liter.

Name _____

National Metric Week
Temperature in °C

Monkey Match

Read each temperature.
Color the thermometer.
Draw a line to match the correct monkey.

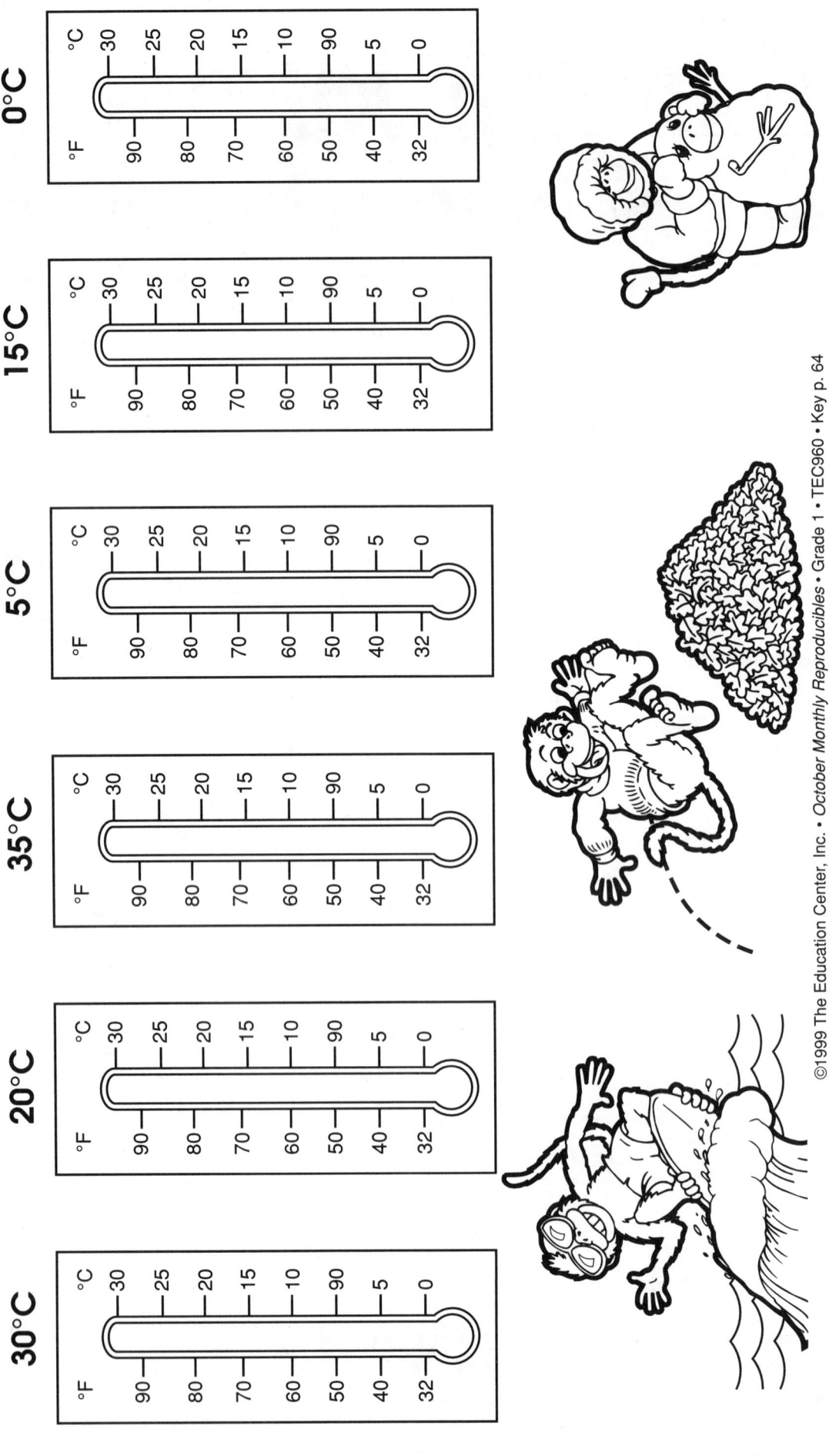

22   ©1999 The Education Center, Inc. • *October Monthly Reproducibles* • Grade 1 • TEC960 • Key p. 64

Name _____

National Metric Week
Linear measurement: centimeters

Just Hangin' Around

Estimate. Write.
Measure. Write.

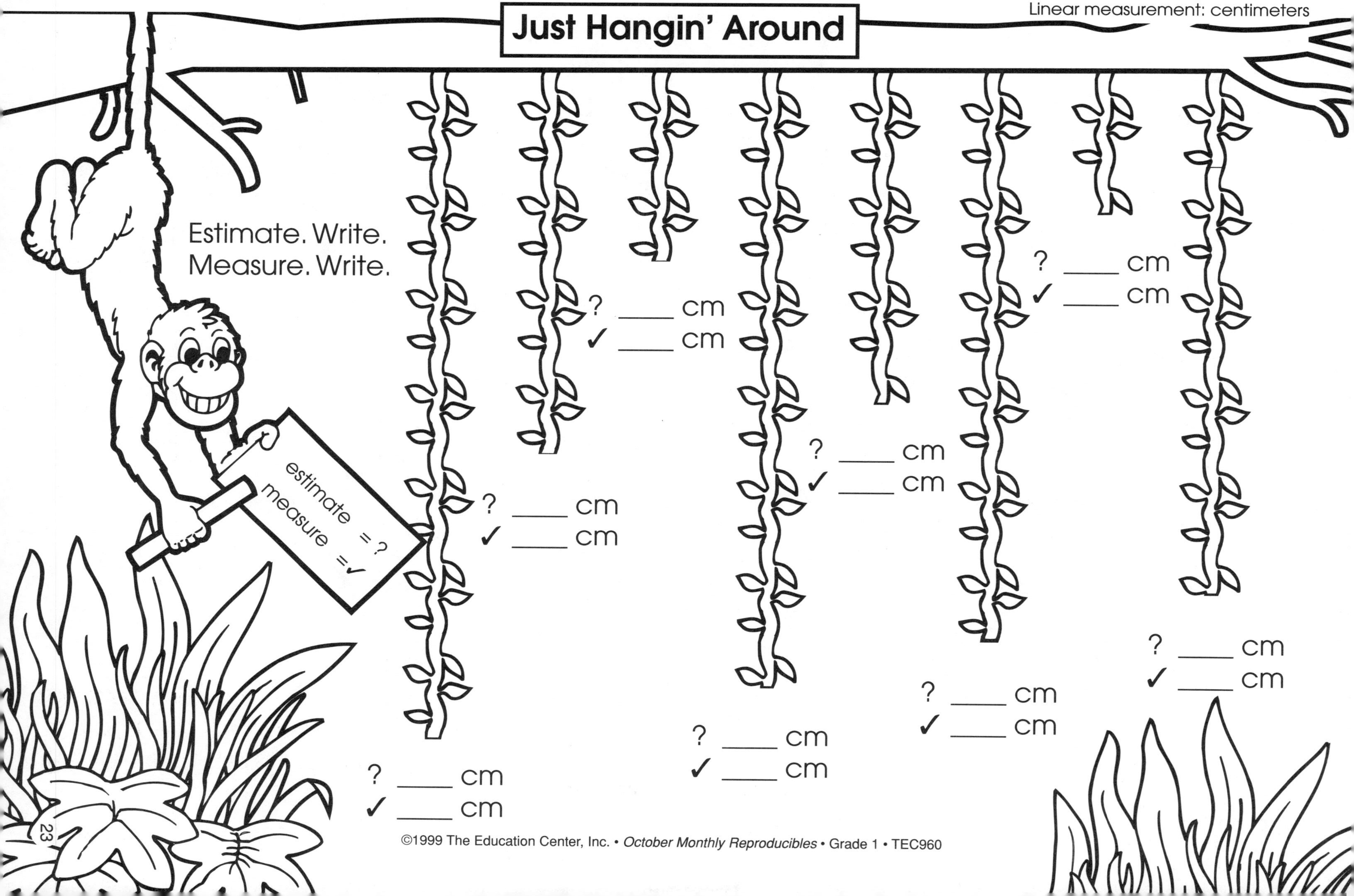

? ___ cm
✓ ___ cm

(repeated for each vine)

estimate = ?
measure = ✓

**National Metric Week
Monkey Pattern**

©1999 The Education Center, Inc. • *October Monthly Reproducibles* • Grade 1 • TEC960

Note To The Teacher: Use with "Monkey Measurement" on page 21.

Columbus Day

Christopher Columbus set sail from Spain on August 3, 1492, in search of a shorter route to the Indies. After several weeks of seeing only a vast ocean, he and his crew reached land on October 12. Though it wasn't the Indies as he was expecting, Columbus had encountered a world that we now call the Americas. Today this landing is recognized annually on October 12.

Sail Into History

With the help of this unique minibook, your students will look forward to reading all about the history of Columbus's famous voyage. To make a booklet, give each child a white construction-paper copy of page 26. Ask each child to color the page as desired; then ask her to cut each of the pieces on the heavy solid lines. To assemble, she sequences and staples the sails. Next she glues the ship and flag to opposite tips of a craft stick. Finally, she glues the sails to the middle of the craft stick as shown. Encourage her to sail into the story of Columbus by reading the text on each of the sails. After you review this rebus story with your youngsters, challenge them to create a story of their own using a rebus format.

Others Discover

Columbus made an important discovery for his people, but each of your students has been a discoverer too. Ask each student to brainstorm a list of things that he learned or discovered on his own that he previously had not known about. Give each child a sheet of drawing paper and have him write about and illustrate a personal discovery. Create a book cover titled "I discovered..." Then bind all the students' drawings to create a class big book of discoveries. Just by reading the book, each child will see that his classmates have discovered some fascinating things.

Columbus Day
Minibook

Columbus set sail from Spain with three 🚢s. He and about 90 👥 sailed across the 〰️.

1

They sailed for months looking for 🏝️. Columbus used the ✨ to find his way.

2

The 👥 finally saw 🏝️. Columbus took 🦜 and 🪙 back to Spain.

3

Columbus had found a new land. We call it America!

4

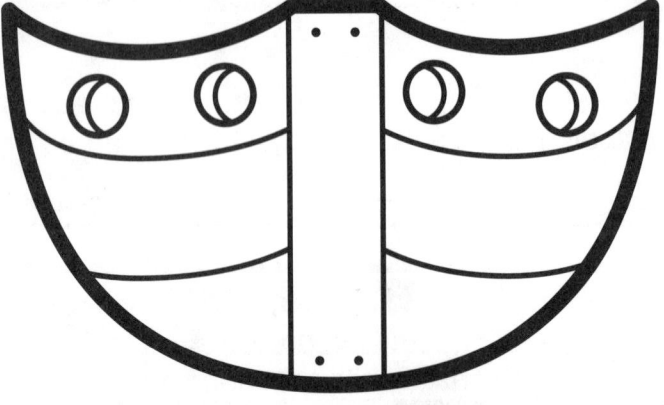

©1999 The Education Center, Inc. • October Monthly Reproducibles • Grade 1 • TEC960

Name _____ Columbus Day
Vocabulary

Columbus's Crew

Name each picture.
Write.
Use the word box.

Word Box

birds   fish
tree   water
cloud   ship

"Land ho!"

Bonus Box: On the back of this sheet, write a sentence using one of these words.

Name _____   Columbus Day
Color words

What A Sight

Read and color.

- yellow
- green
- black
- red
- black
- brown
- orange
- purple
- brown
- yellow
- blue
- orange
- purple
- blue
- brown
- brown
- blue

28   ©1999 The Education Center, Inc. • *October Monthly Reproducibles* • Grade 1 • TEC960

HAPPY BIRTHDAY, Steven Kellogg!

Steven Kellogg began drawing and telling stories at an early age. He spent much of his spare time creating drawings of animals and birds, which he displayed proudly on his bedroom walls. Later this hobby would lead him to illustrate more than 90 stories—some of which he also authored. Honor this famed children's author and illustrator on his birthday, October 26.

A Cake For Kellogg

Cut a large sheet of bulletin-board paper to resemble a cake, add birthday candle cutouts, and display it on a classroom wall. After sharing several of Kellogg's stories, ask each child to illustrate a Kellogg character on the cake shape. Use the completed mural for a backdrop as you pay tribute to Steven Kellogg during a class birthday celebration on October 26.

Who's The Illustrator?

After becoming familiar with Steven Kellogg's illustrations, your students will enjoy this challenge. Gather about 15 children's books—seven of which should be illustrated by Kellogg. Carefully mask the author and illustrator information on all of the books; then display them in your classroom. Encourage each child to visit the display, look through the books, and then write the titles of the books he thinks were illustrated by Kellogg. When everyone has had a chance to take part, reveal Kellogg's creations as each child reviews his selections.

Kellogg's Creations

This assortment of stories features just a few of the books illustrated by Kellogg. Use this list to introduce your students to his extraordinary work.

A My Name Is Alice by Jane Bayer (Puffin Books, 1995)
Can I Keep Him? by Steven Kellogg (Dial Books For Young Readers, 1971)
Pecos Bill by Steven Kellogg (Morrow Junior Books, 1992)
Tallyho, Pinkerton! by Steven Kellogg (Dial Books For Young Readers, 1982)
The Day Jimmy's Boa Ate The Wash by Trinka Hakes Noble (Dial Books For Young Readers, 1980)
The Island Of The Skog by Steven Kellogg (Puffin Books, 1993)
Yankee Doodle by Edward Bangs (Simon & Schuster Books For Young Readers, 1996)

Name _____

Happy Birthday, Steven Kellogg!
Story map

What's The Story?

Characters

Setting

Title

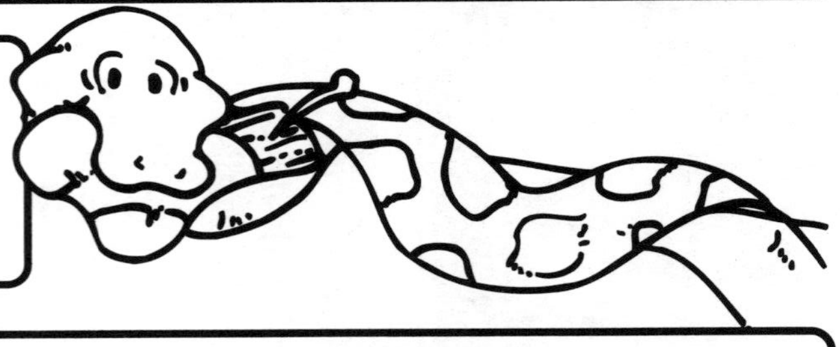

Problem

Solution

©1998 The Education Center, Inc. • *October Monthly Reproducibles* • Grade 1 • TEC960

Note To The Teacher: Use this page as a whole-class review or as an individual book response. Use it with any Steven Kellogg book.

Name_____ Happy Birthday, Steven Kellogg!
Can I Keep Him?/Comprehension

Animals Wanted

Read each sentence.
Write in the missing word.
Use the Word Bank.

Can I keep him?

No, dear!

🐕	Dogs _____ all the time.
🐈	Kittens grow _____.
🦌	Bucks have sharp _____.
🐻	Bears _____.
🐅	Tigers eat too much _____.
🐍	Pythons shed their _____.
🦕	Dinosaurs can not be _____.
👦	Ralph will _____ with you.

Word Bank: food   smell   pets   play
　　　　　　　 fur   antlers   bark   skin

Bonus Box: Color the animal you would like to keep.

©1999 The Education Center, Inc. • *October Monthly Reproducibles* • Grade 1 • TEC960 • Key p. 64

Note To The Teacher: Obtain a copy of *Can I Keep Him?* and read it aloud before having students complete this activity.

31

Name _____

Pinkerton's Path

Happy Birthday, Steven Kellogg!
Tallyho, Pinkerton!/Story sequence

Cut and glue the pictures in order.

① ② ③ ④ ⑤ ⑥

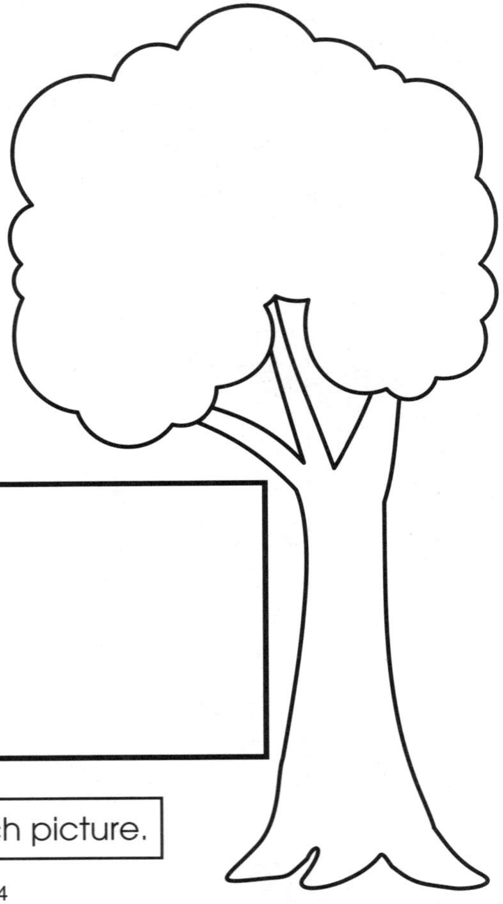

Bonus Box: On the back of this sheet, write a sentence to go with each picture.

©1999 The Education Center, Inc. • *October Monthly Reproducibles* • Grade 1 • TEC960 • Key p. 64

Note To The Teacher: Obtain a copy of *Tallyho, Pinkerton!* and read it aloud to introduce this activity.

32

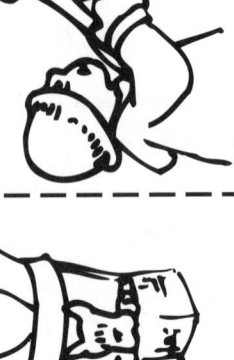

SPIDERS

Spin a sensational study of spiders with this wonderful web of ideas.

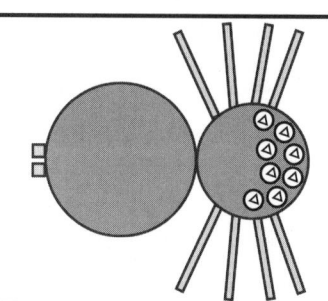

Busy Bodies
Familiarize your students with the characteristics of spiders by sharing the following information. A spider is a member of the *arachnid* family and has two main body parts—the first of which is called the *cephalothorax*. It has eight legs that are attached to the cephalothorax. Most spiders have eight eyes, and all can spin silk, which some spiders use to spin webs. A spider's spinnerets lie at the back of the second body part, or *abdomen*.

Now review these body parts with this easy-to-implement art project that reinforces listening skills and geometric shapes. Distribute a sheet of drawing paper and crayons to each child. Give the following instructions one at a time for students to follow:

— Draw a circle the size of a tennis ball for the spider's *cephalothorax*.
— Draw four thin rectangles on each side of the cephalothorax to make legs.
— Draw a slightly larger circle for the abdomen.
— Draw two small squares at the back of the abdomen for the spinnerets.
— Draw eight small circles on the cephalothorax for the eyes.
— Draw a tiny triangle inside of each eye.

Display these spectacular spider drawings for all to enjoy.

Caught In The Web
Use this wonderful web display to reinforce a host of basic skills. To prepare, staple or pin white yarn in the shape of a spider web to a bulletin board. Select a skill such as beginning sounds, sums of ten, rhyming words, or opposites. Write the selected skill on a spider cutout and place it in the center of the web. Duplicate a class supply of simple bug patterns and distribute one to each student. Instruct him to program his bug with an example of the targeted skill. Attach the programmed bugs to the web for an eye-catching review.

Name _____

Spiders
Rhyming words

Spider Rhymes

Find a rhyme for each web.
Cut. Glue.

Bonus Box: On the back of this sheet, write the words for six of these pictures.

©1999 The Education Center, Inc. • *October Monthly Reproducibles* • Grade 1 • TEC960

34

Name _____

Spiders
Reading comprehension

See The Spider!

Read.
Find a picture for each bold word.
Cut and glue.
Draw the spider to match each sentence.

1. See the spider by the **cat**.

2. See the spider on the **hat**.

3. See the spider in the **house**.

4. See the spider under the **mouse**.

5. See the spider above the **car**.

6. See the spider in the **jar**.

©1999 The Education Center, Inc. • October Monthly Reproducibles • Grade 1 • TEC960

35

HAPPY HALLOWEEN!

If your students are talking about tricks and treats, you know that Halloween is fast approaching! Capture the attention of your little goblins with these fun activities that combine basic skills practice with the magic of Halloween.

Halloween Sort

Enjoy many elements of Halloween by engaging your students in this special sorting activity. Assemble a collection of Halloween-related items, such as wrapped candy, parts of costumes, pumpkins, flashlights, books, pictures, and toys. Invite your class to sit in a circle on the floor while you show each item and discuss its connection to Halloween. Then encourage students to sort the items by purpose, color, size, or other meaningful ways. When your whole-group activity ends, store the items in a trick-or-treat bag for further exploration in a learning center.

Trick-Or-Treat Surprise

This writing activity will be a real treat for your students. Give each child a white construction-paper copy of page 42 and a paper lunch bag. Provide access to glue and a variety of art materials. Begin by discussing some fun and creative things that a child might find in her trick-or-treat bag on Halloween night. After several suggestions have been shared, ask each child to imagine finding something amazing in her own trick-or-treat bag. Have her write a description of the item on her paper. Then have her color the two pieces and cut them out on the heavy, solid outlines. Assist her in gluing the writing to the front of the paper bag and the character to the inside rim of the bag as shown. Finally, have her use the provided art materials to create the object she described in her writing; then have her place the completed creation inside the bag. Display the finished projects on a bulletin board as a special treat for everyone to enjoy.

I was so surprised when I looked in my treat bag! I found…

Name

Name_____ Happy Halloween!
Sets to 12

Candy Count

Circle matching sets of candy.
Count.
Write each amount.

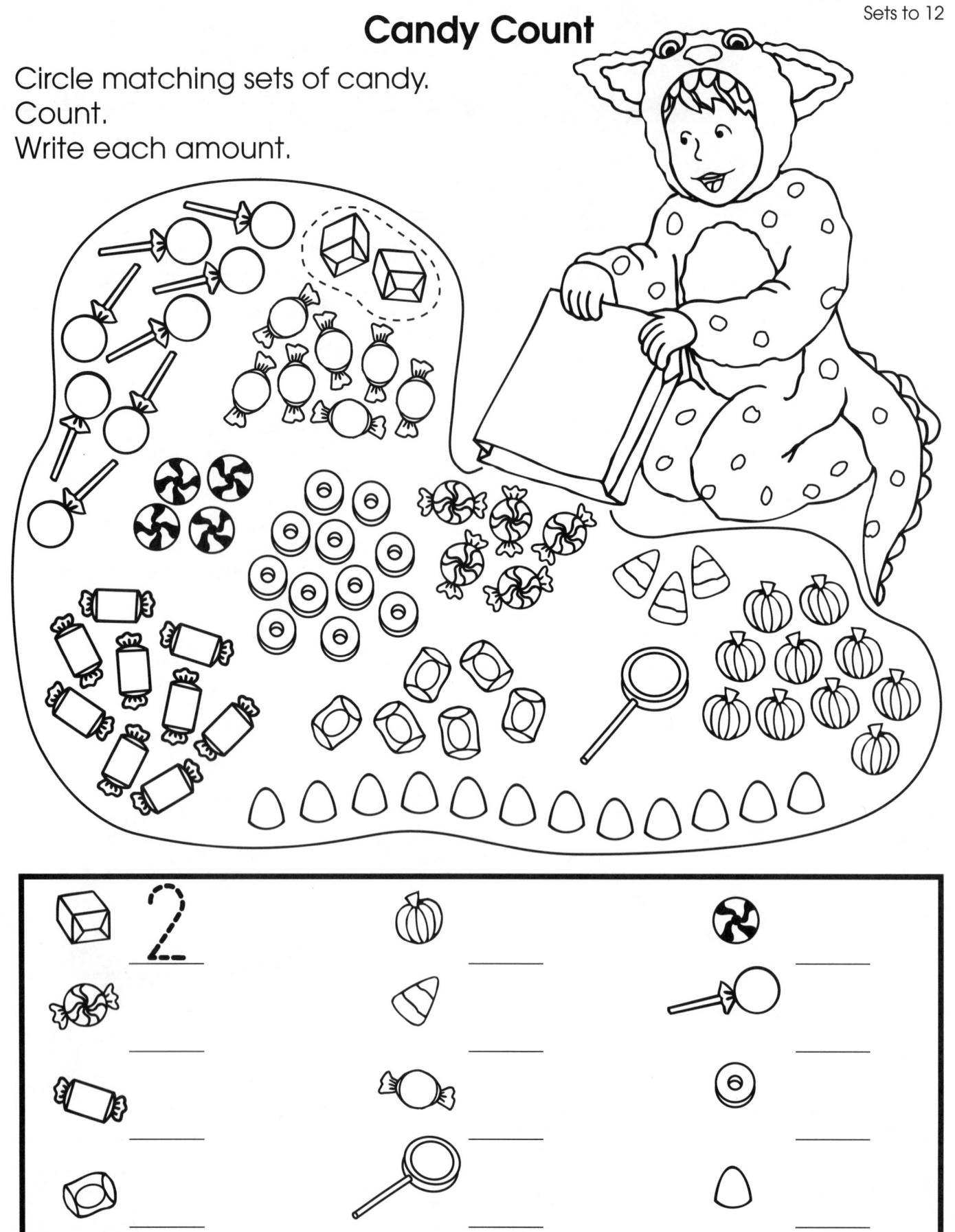

Name_____

Happy Halloween!
Sets to 8

Trick-Or-Treat Totals

Draw.
Add.

3 + 3

2 + 6

3 + 4

5 + 1

8 + 0

2 + 5

4 + 4

4 + 2

2 + 3

1 + 7

3 + 5

©1999 The Education Center, Inc. • *October Monthly Reproducibles* • Grade 1 • TEC960

Happy Halloween!
Alphabet recognition

Name _____

Dots Of Fun

Connect the dots in ABC order.
Color.

©1999 The Education Center, Inc. • *October Monthly Reproducibles* • Grade 1 • TEC960

Name_____

Happy Halloween!
Patterning

Sweet Treats

Cut and glue to complete each pattern.

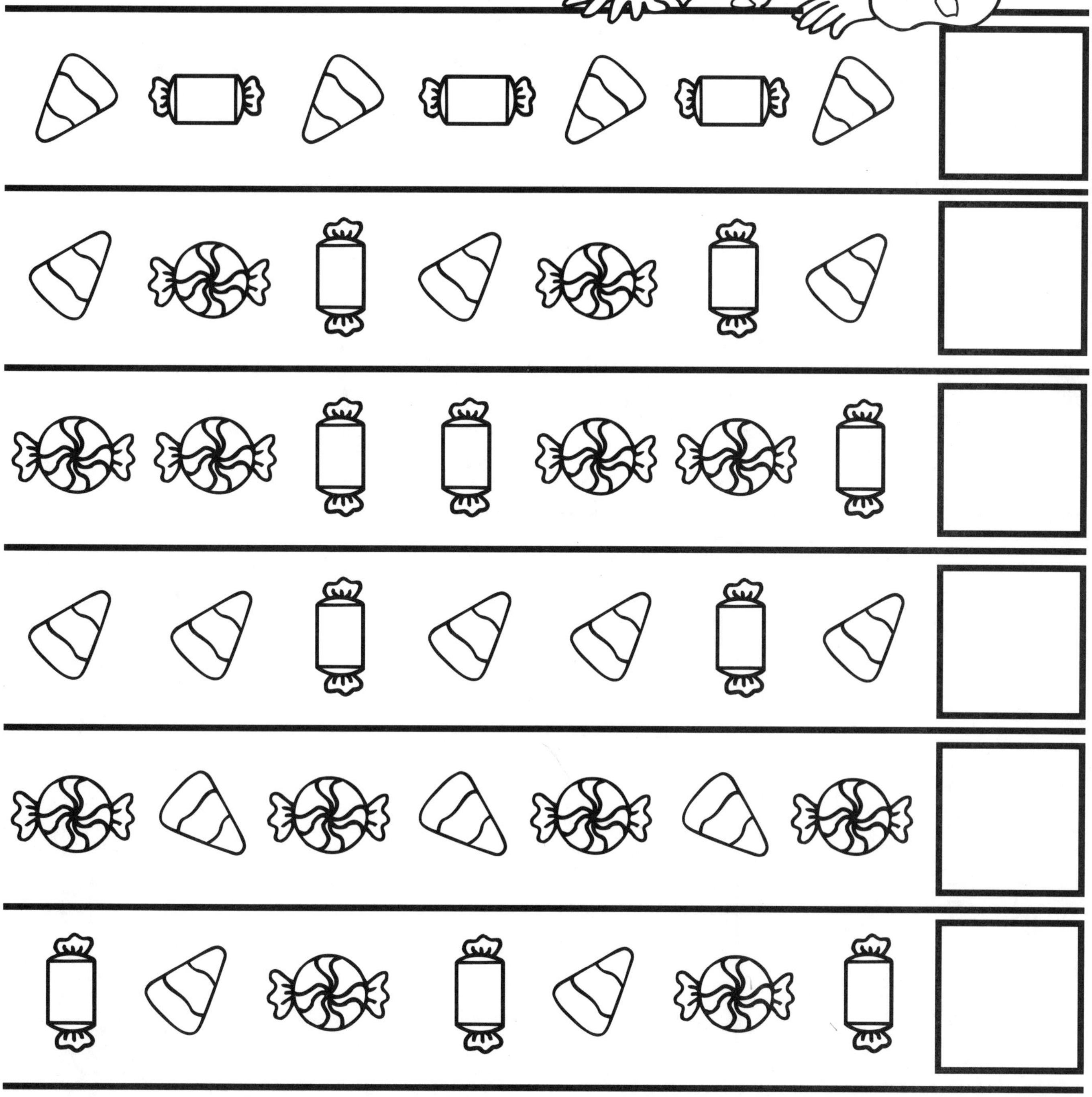

©1999 The Education Center, Inc. • *October Monthly Reproducibles* • Grade 1 • TEC960

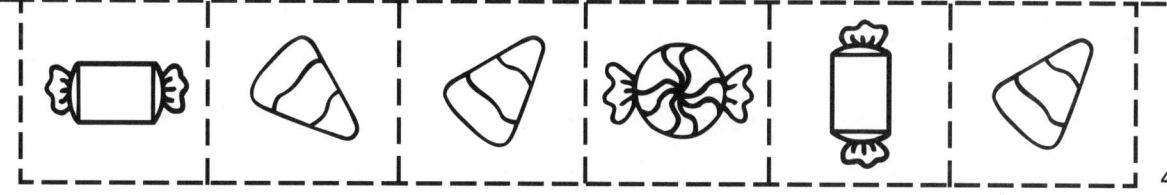

41

Happy Halloween!
Creative writing

©1999 The Education Center, Inc. • October Monthly Reproducibles • Grade 1 • TEC960

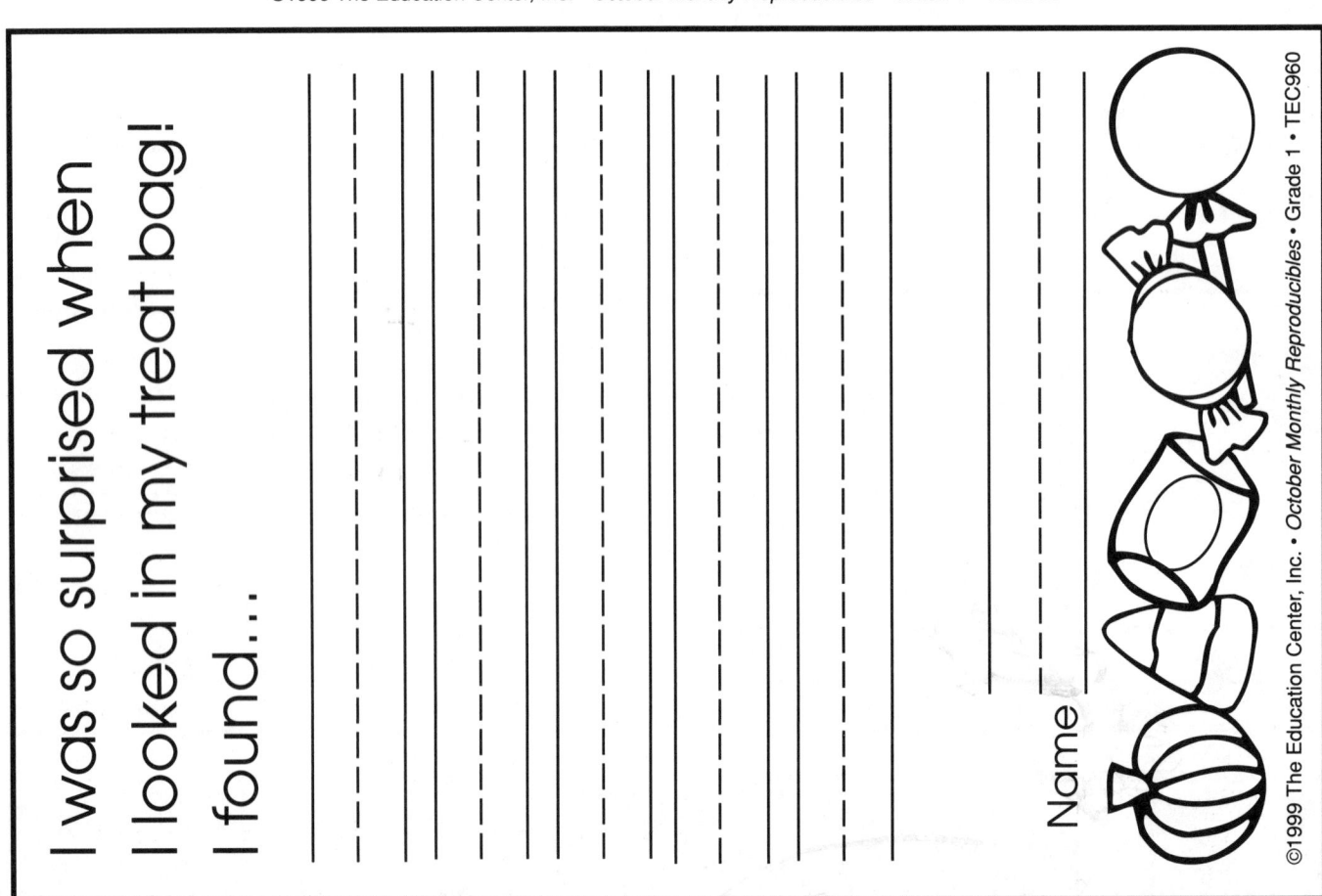

I was so surprised when I looked in my treat bag! I found...

Name _____

Note To The Teacher: Use with "Trick-Or-Treat Surprise" on page 37.

NATIONAL PIZZA MONTH

No matter how you slice it, pizza is an all-time favorite treat! Create an appetizing atmosphere for National Pizza Month, observed in October, with these tempting activities.

Pizza To Go
Get your students on the move with this appetizing addition activity. In advance, prepare a class set of tagboard cutouts that resemble slices of pizza. Attach from one to nine red, self-stick dots (pepperoni) to each slice. Distribute a slice to each student. At your signal, instruct each child to find a buddy and add the pepperoni on their slices. Ask each pair to identify the number sentence made by their slices and the corresponding answer. Then have each child find a new partner for another round of play. For an added challenge, have students work in groups of three to add larger sums. Ready for a slice to go?

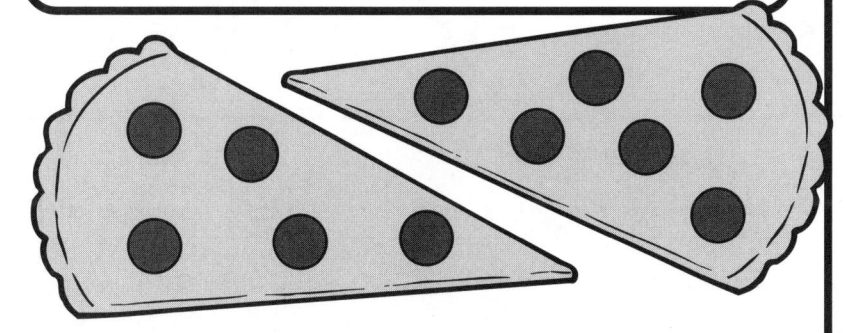

Perky Pizza Prints
These perky prints make a display that looks good enough to eat! To make a pizza print, give each student a triangle cut from red construction paper. Provide an assortment of halved vegetables—such as green peppers, mushrooms, and onions—and shallow dishes of orange, green, brown, and yellow tempera paints. Instruct the student to press a vegetable slice into a dish of paint and then press the image onto his triangle. Have him repeat the procedure using different shapes and colors. Allow the prints to dry; then display them on a bulletin board covered in yellow paper. Add the title "Pizza, Anyone?" and be prepared to attract a hungry crowd!

Name _____

National Pizza Month
Logic

It's A Pizza Party!

Read the clues.
Circle the special slice.

It has 🥦. 
It does not have 🍄.

It does not have 🍕. 
It has 🫑.

It has ⭕. 
It has 🍄.

It has 🥦. 
It has 🫑.

Bonus Box: On the back of this sheet, write a sentence about your favorite pizza toppings.

©1999 The Education Center, Inc. • October Monthly Reproducibles • Grade 1 • TEC960

Name _____

National Pizza Month
Sequencing

Let's Make A Pizza!

Pizza tastes great!
It's fun to make, too.

Cut.
Glue in order.

① Roll the dough.   ②   ③   ④   ⑤

Bonus Box: On the back of this sheet, draw your favorite kind of pizza.

©1999 The Education Center, Inc. • *October Monthly Reproducibles* • Grade 1 • TEC960

Eat! | Bake in the oven. | Spread the sauce. | Add the toppings.

45

Name _____

National Pizza Month
Classification

In The Kitchen

Cut.
Sort.
Glue.

Pizza Tools

Pizza Toppings

©1999 The Education Center, Inc. • October Monthly Reproducibles • Grade 1 • TEC960

| mushroom | spoon | mitt | pepperoni | pepper | pan | cutter | onion |

46

Name _____

National Pizza Month
Addition to 7

More Pizza, Please!

Count.
Add.

1. 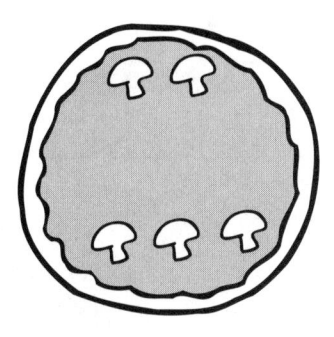 2 + 3 = ____

2. 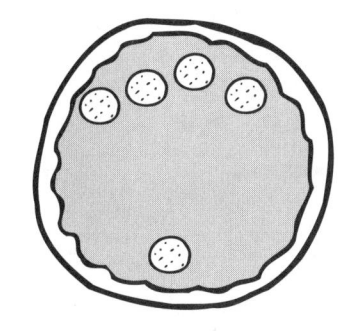 4 + 1 = ____

3.  1 + 3 = ____

4. 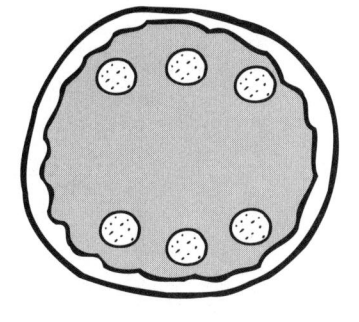 3 + 3 = ____

5.  5 + 1 = ____

6. 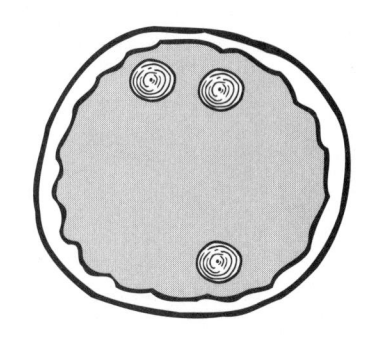 2 + 1 = ____

7.  3 + 0 = ____

8. 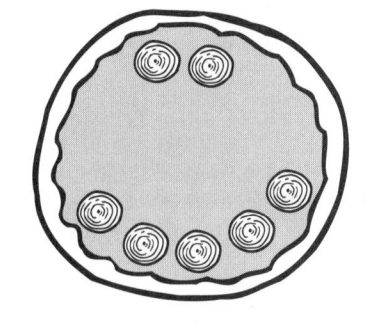 2 + 5 = ____

9.  3 + 4 = ____

Draw to match.
Add.

10.  4 + 2 = ____

11.  6 + 1 = ____

©1999 The Education Center, Inc. • *October Monthly Reproducibles* • Grade 1 • TEC960

Name _____

National Pizza Month
Subtraction to 8

By The Slice

Cut.
Use the slices to help you subtract.
Write.

5 − 2 = _____   8 − 4 = _____

6 − 4 = _____   7 − 2 = _____

8 − 2 = _____   4 − 3 = _____

4 − 2 = _____   7 − 6 = _____

7 − 3 = _____   8 − 8 = _____

3 − 3 = _____   6 − 3 = _____

©1999 The Education Center, Inc. • October Monthly Reproducibles • Grade 1 • TEC960

NATIONAL POPCORN POPPIN' MONTH

Oh, for the love of popcorn! You won't have any trouble finding eager volunteers to help you celebrate this monthlong event honoring a much-loved snack!

Poppin' Word Practice

Here's a tasty way to start off your popcorn unit! In advance, cut out at least a class supply of popcorn shapes from white construction paper. Begin by asking your class to watch as you make a fresh batch of popcorn. (An oil or air popper will work best for this demonstration.) As you proceed through the steps, encourage your students to notice sights, smells, and sounds. When the batch has popped, invite each child to touch and taste a portion of the popcorn. Next ask each child to tell you a popcorn-related word that was inspired by the demonstration. Write each word on a separate popcorn cutout. Store the words in a pocket chart for a quick reference during a popcorn-related writing activity, such as "Popcorn Punctuation" on this page.

Popcorn Punctuation

It can be quite a challenge to get first graders to use periods at the end of their written sentences. Try using this activity to help them remember to punctuate. Give a copy of page 52 to each student, along with a few unpopped popcorn kernels. Encourage each child to write a creative story or descriptive paragraph with a popcorn theme. Then have her glue a popcorn kernel atop each period. The next time your students take on a writing assignment, punctuation will "pop" to mind more readily!

The ABCs Of Popcorn

Treat your youngsters to this alphabetizing activity. In advance, write the letters A through Z from left to right across a chalkboard. Then give five children a labeled popcorn cutout from your class-created set. (See "Poppin' Word Practice" on this page.) Ask each child with a cutout to identify the beginning letter of the word he was given, and have him stand facing the corresponding letter on the chalkboard. After each child has found his position, have him turn to face the class, holding the card so the word is visible to the other children. Ask your students to read the words from left to right. Emphasize that they are in alphabetical order. Repeat the activity several times using different words and students. Finally, remove the lettering from the chalkboard, and challenge a set of students with cutouts to assemble themselves alphabetically without the visual aid.

Name_____ National Popcorn Poppin' Month
Initial consonants: j, q, v, y, z

j q v y z

Say each picture name.
Write the beginning letter.

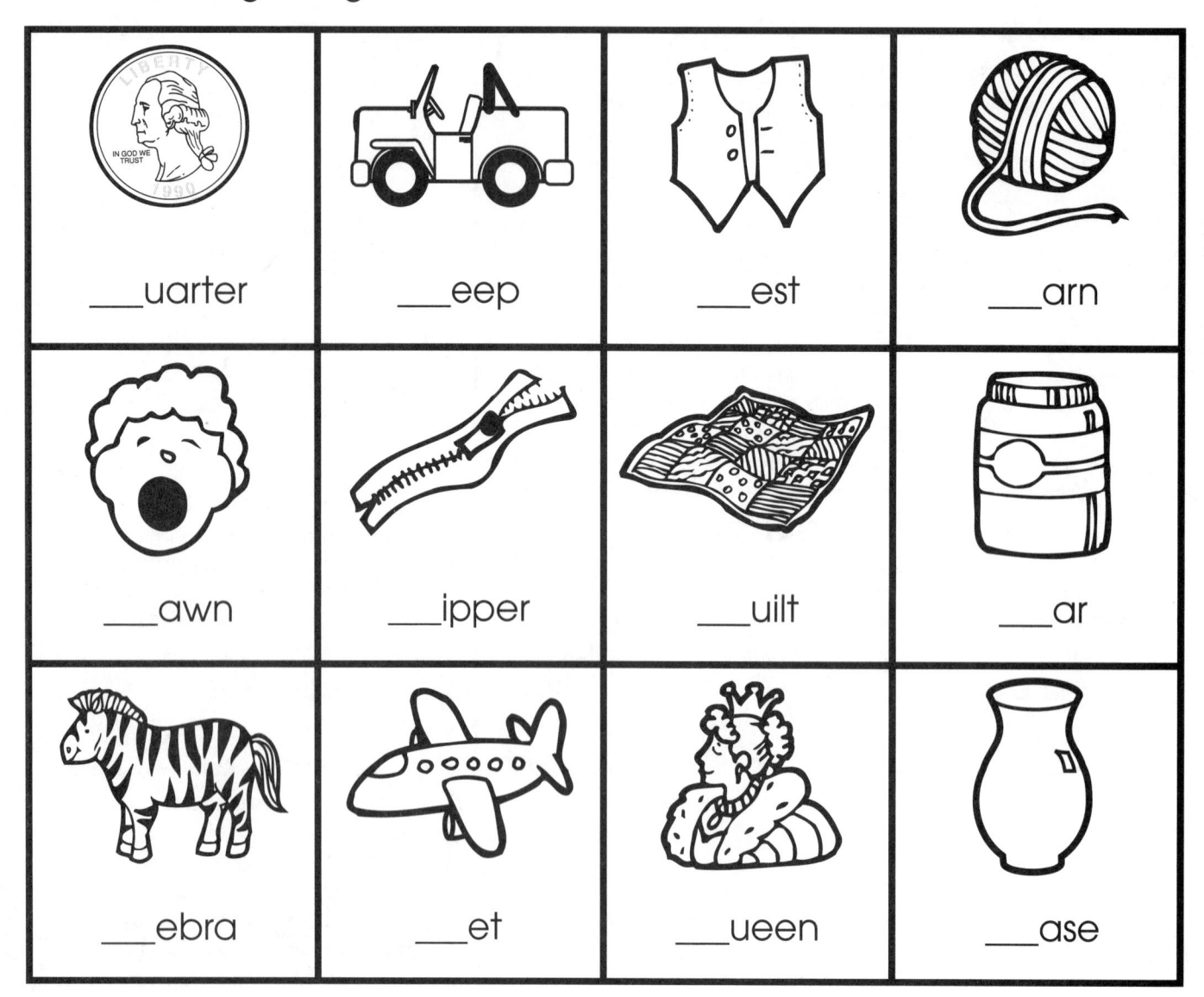

___uarter	___eep	___est	___arn
___awn	___ipper	___uilt	___ar
___ebra	___et	___ueen	___ase

Color each box by the code.

j = red   q = yellow   v = blue   y = green   z = orange

50 ©1999 The Education Center, Inc. • October Monthly Reproducibles • Grade 1 • TEC960

Name_____

National Popcorn Poppin' Month
Number recognition to 25

Number Crunching

Write the missing numbers in order.

1, __, __, __, __
__, 7, __, __, 10
__, __, __, 14, __
16, __, __, __, __
__, 22, __, __, __

©1999 The Education Center, Inc. • October Monthly Reproducibles • Grade 1 • TEC960

Name_____

National Popcorn Poppin' Month
Creative writing

Name _____

National Popcorn Poppin' Month
Rhyming words

Snack In A Sack

Color Code

green
red
blue
yellow
orange

Find the pictures that rhyme.
Color by the code.

Name _____

National Popcorn Poppin' Month
ABC order

Order Of Popcorn

Circle the letter that comes first in ABC order.

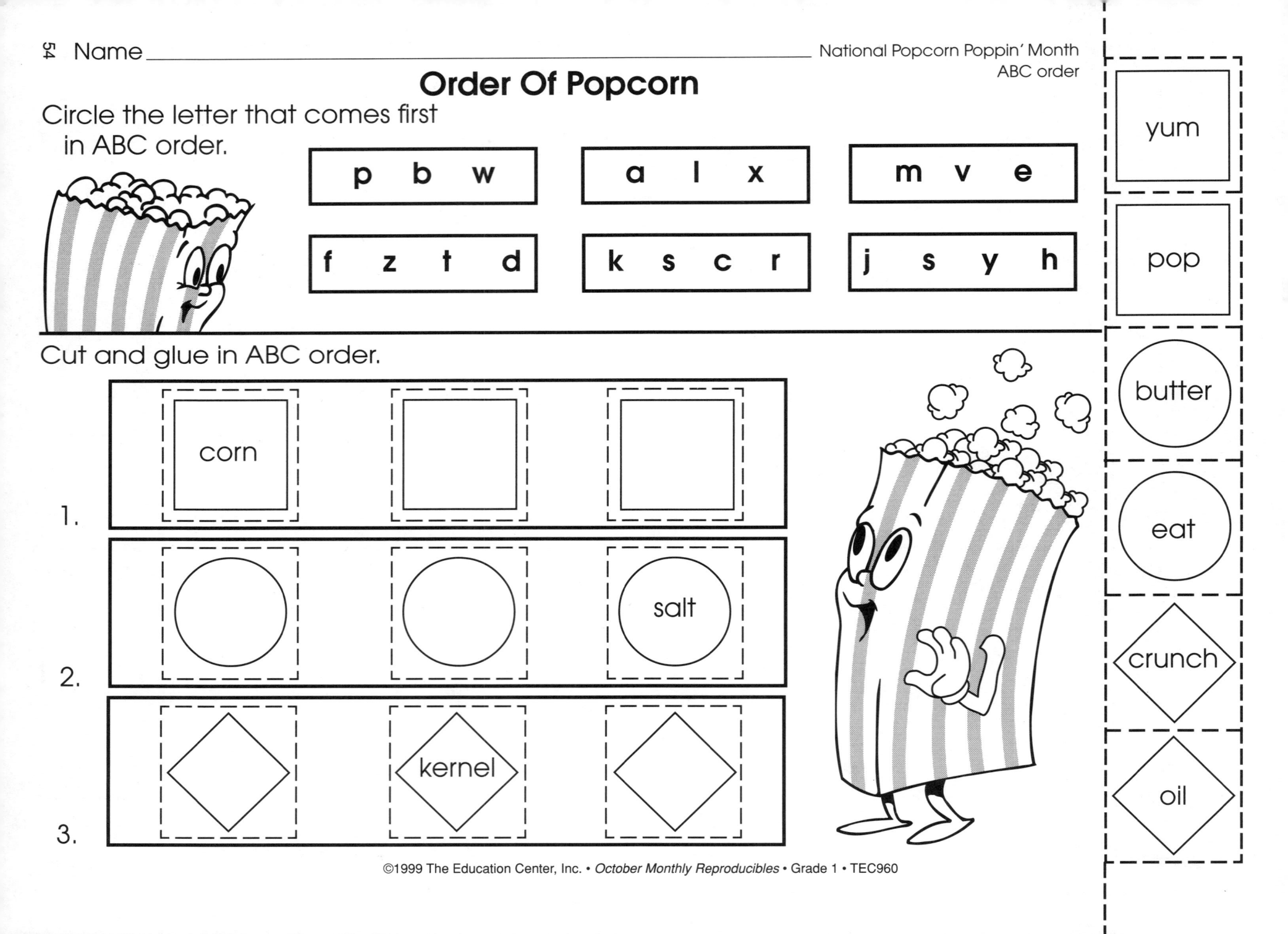

| p b w | a l x | m v e |

| f z t d | k s c r | j s y h |

Cut and glue in ABC order.

1.
2.
3.

---

yum | pop | butter | eat | crunch | oil

corn | salt | kernel

54

©1999 The Education Center, Inc. • October Monthly Reproducibles • Grade 1 • TEC960

NATIONAL COOKIE MONTH

It's National Cookie Month, and that means it's time to take to the kitchen to whip up a batch of your favorite cookies. The captivating activities and reproducibles in this unit are a sweet way to treat your students to some basic skills practice.

COOKIE-CUTTER COUNTERS

Your students will love the hands-on component in this math center. In advance, cut cookie shapes from construction paper and write a different addition problem on each cookie. Program the sum on the back of the cutout. Place the prepared "cookies" in a cookie jar; then add an assortment of cookie cutters (at least as many as your largest sum) to the center. A child takes a cookie from the jar and uses cookie cutters as manipulatives to solve the addition sentence. She then checks her answer with the sum on the back of the cutout. As a tasty finale, treat each child to a cookie after she completes the center. Yum!

JOURNAL TREATS

Your students will think this journal activity is a treat. To make a journal for each child, place several sheets of manuscript paper between a construction-paper copy of the journal cover (on page 56) and a blank sheet of construction paper. Staple where indicated; then trim the journal cover and pages along the heavy, solid outline on the journal's cover. Throughout your cookie unit, give your students writing prompts related to cookies, and have them create stories on the pages of their journals. You could also have them record cookie-related vocabulary, story titles, or recipes. When each child has completed his journal, reward him with a cookie before sending his writing home to be enjoyed by his family.

National Cookie Month
Journal Cover

COOKIES

by _____

©1999 The Education Center, Inc. • *October Monthly Reproducibles* • Grade 1 • TEC960

Note To The Teacher: Use with "Journal Treats" on page 55.

Name_____

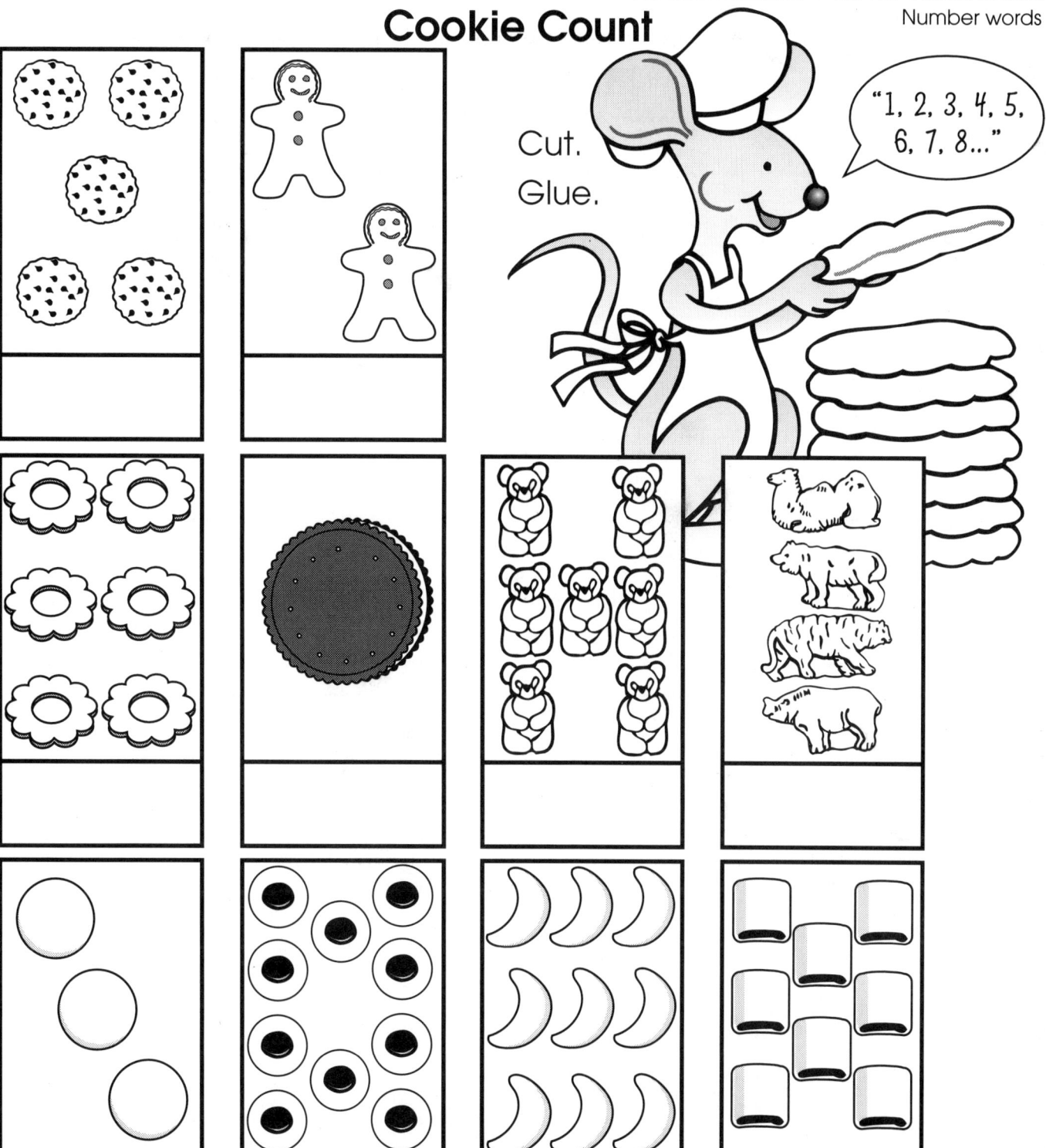

National Cookie Month
Number words

Cookie Count

Cut.
Glue.

"1, 2, 3, 4, 5, 6, 7, 8..."

©1999 The Education Center, Inc. • *October Monthly Reproducibles* • Grade 1 • TEC960

| one | two | three | four | five |
| six | seven | eight | nine | ten |

Name_____ National Cookie Month
Addition to 7

Yummy Sums

How many cookies in all?
Write.

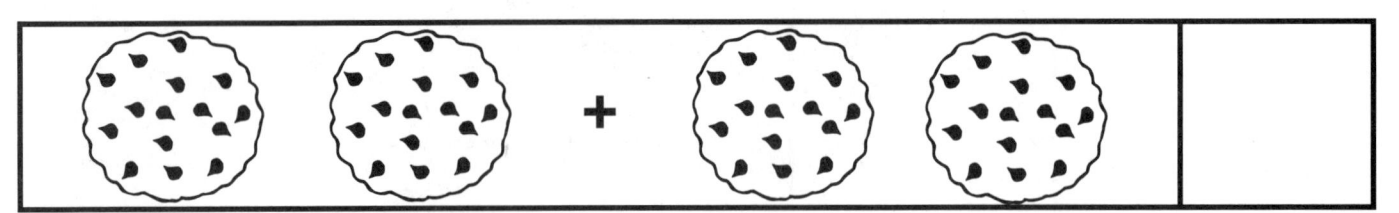

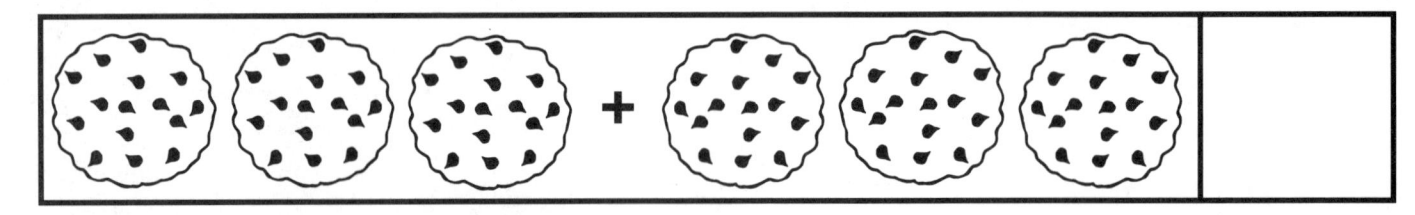

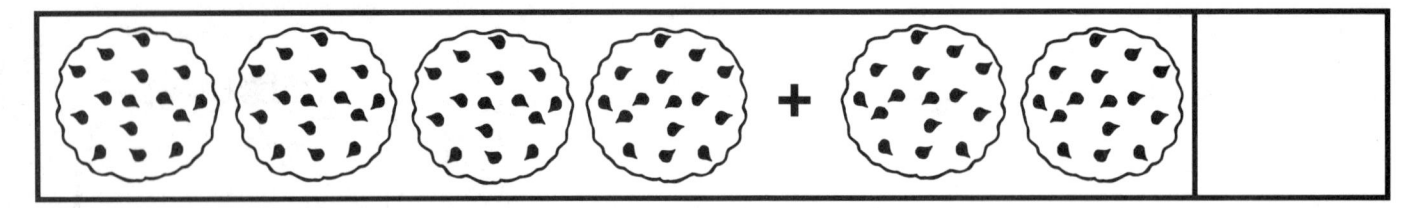

Cut out the cookies. Use them to help you add.

2 + 3 = ☐   7 + 0 = ☐

3 + 4 = ☐   2 + 4 = ☐

2 + 5 = ☐   1 + 6 = ☐

©1999 The Education Center, Inc. • *October Monthly Reproducibles* • Grade 1 • TEC960

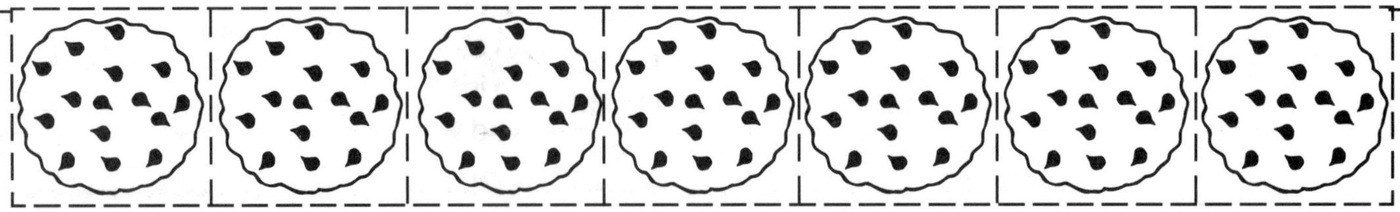

COMPUTER LEARNING MONTH

Take a turn for technology during the month of October as you celebrate Computer Learning Month with your youngsters. This event provides a time to share innovative uses of computers and software. So download some fun with this "tech-rific" selection of reproducibles and awards.

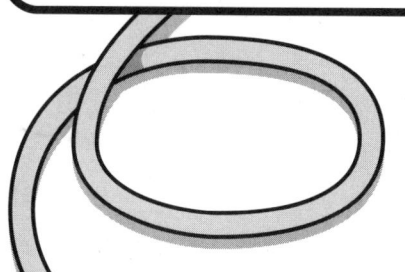

Computer Keepsakes

This easy-to-implement journaling technique will improve students' writing, keyboarding, and computer skills. Each week, have each child use a computer and word-processing program to type a few sentences about school events and current studies. Be sure he dates each entry. Help him save his work on a personalized disk and store the disks in a safe location when not in use. Near the end of the year, have each child print out all of his journal entries and bind them to create a keepsake journal packed with memories of the school year and evidence of his personal writing progress.

Encyclopedia Investigation

Improve your students' researching skills with this intriguing activity. In advance, search a computerized version of an encyclopedia for information related to a unit your students are currently studying. As you search the program, jot down questions that can be answered by accessing information in the electronic encyclopedia. Distribute a copy of the questions to each student; then encourage him to answer each question by locating the information in the electronic encyclopedia. This inspiring research method will have your students asking for more questions to investigate.

Name _____

How's That Compute?

Add.
Write each sum on the screen.
Color by the code.

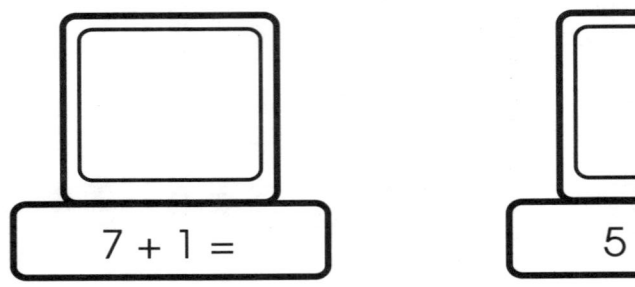

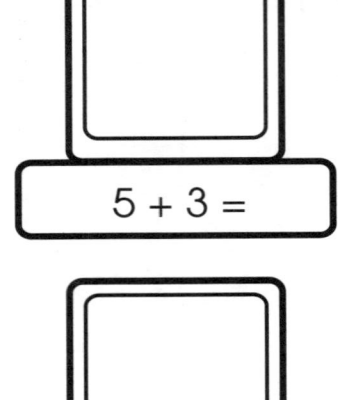

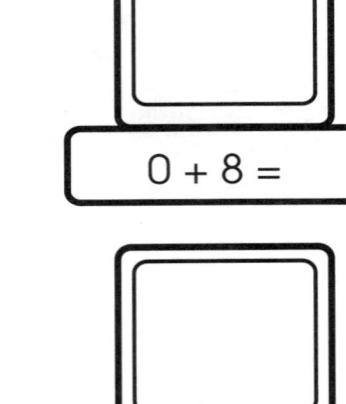

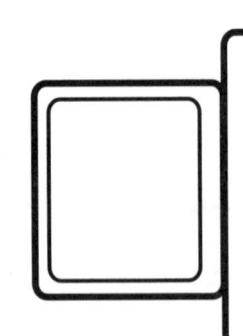

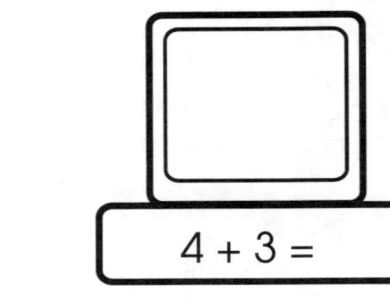

7 + 1 =

3 + 2 =

6 + 2 =

5 + 3 =

6 + 1 =

5 + 1 =

0 + 8 =

5 + 2 =

2 + 4 =

4 + 3 =

3 + 1 =

Color Code: even number = green
odd number = blue

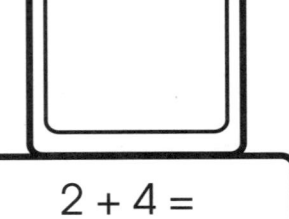

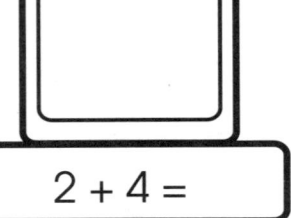

©1999 The Education Center, Inc. • *October Monthly Reproducibles* • Grade 1 • TEC960

Computer Learning Month
Sums to 8

Name _____

Computer Learning Month
Number words/numerals

Downloading Numbers

Cut.
Match.

one | four | two | five | three | six | eight | seven | nine | ten

10 | 7 | 6 | 8 | 3 | 1 | 4 | 2 | 5 | 9

Note To The Teacher: Have each child cut out the strips. Assist each child with cutting along each of the four broken lines on the screen. Insert the strips in the openings so that one numeral and one number word show. Have each child pull to match.

Name _____   Computer Learning Month
Computer-use contract

Computer Contract

I will do my best to be a responsible computer user!

☐ I will keep food and drinks away from the computer.

☐ I will handle the keyboard and mouse gently.

☐ I will respect all computer users.

_____
(signed)

©1999 The Education Center, Inc. • *October Monthly Reproducibles* • Grade 1 • TEC960

Note To The Teacher: Give each child a copy of the contract. Read each sentence aloud. Ask each student to put a check mark in each box as the sentence is read. Have him sign the contract after he agrees to the rules. Display the contracts near your classroom computer center.

Computer Learning Month
Awards

(student)

**is entitled
to this
computer award
for**

signed: _____

©1999 The Education Center, Inc. • *October Monthly Reproducibles* • Grade 1 • TEC960

**Computer Congrats
are awarded to**

_____!
(student)

_____
(signed)

_____
(date)

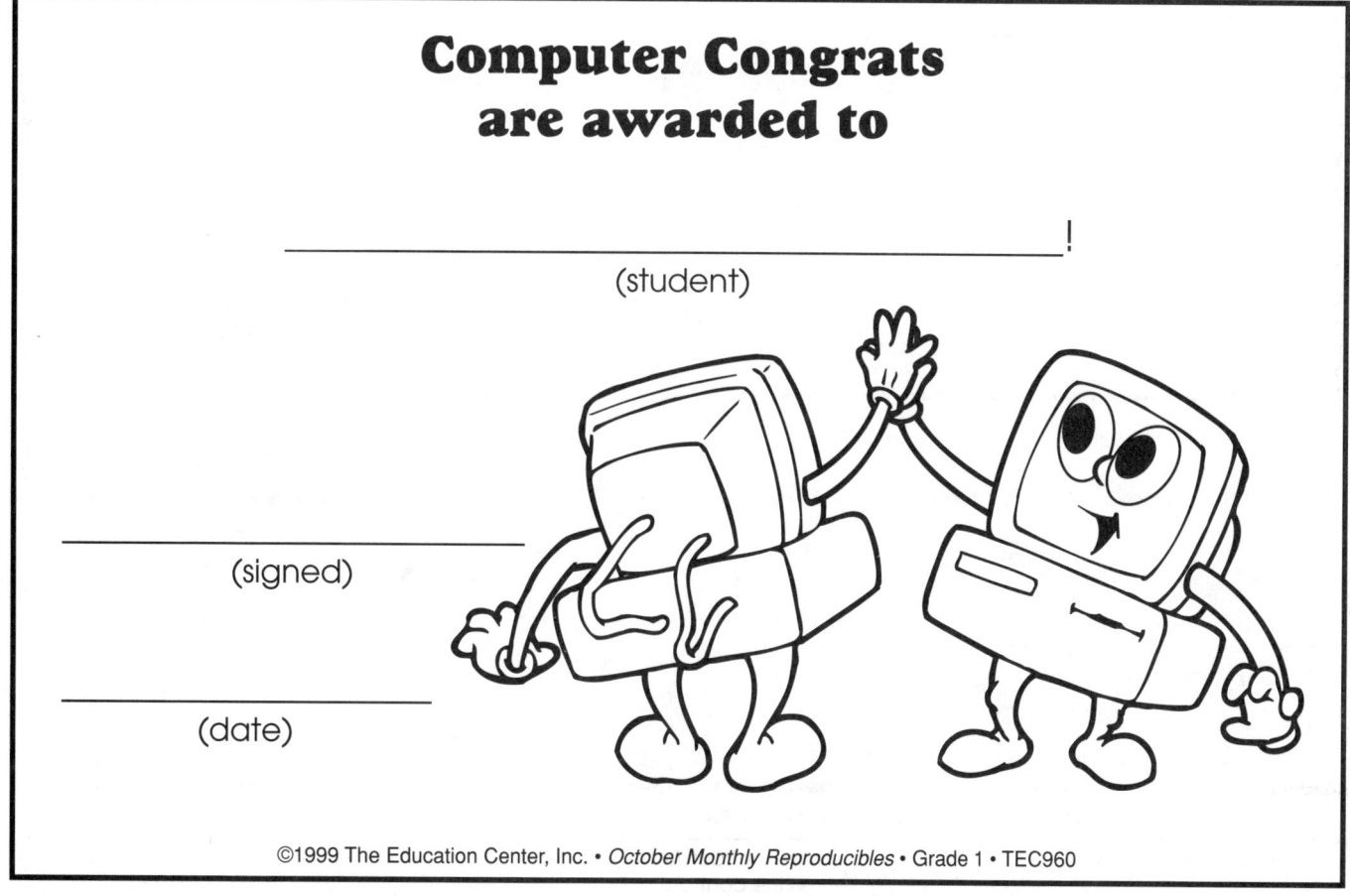

©1999 The Education Center, Inc. • *October Monthly Reproducibles* • Grade 1 • TEC960

Answer Keys

Page 22

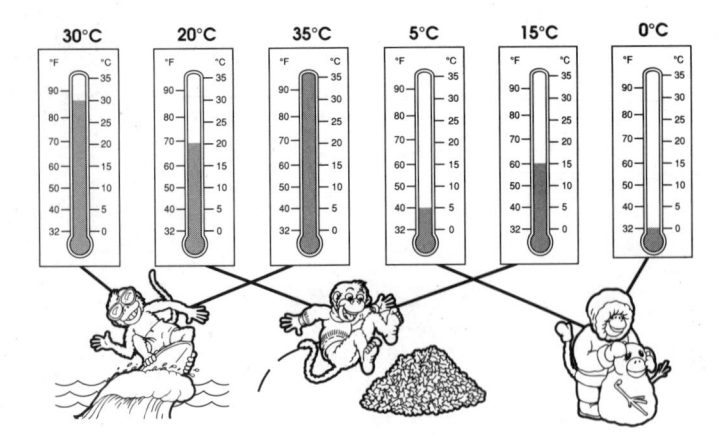

Page 31

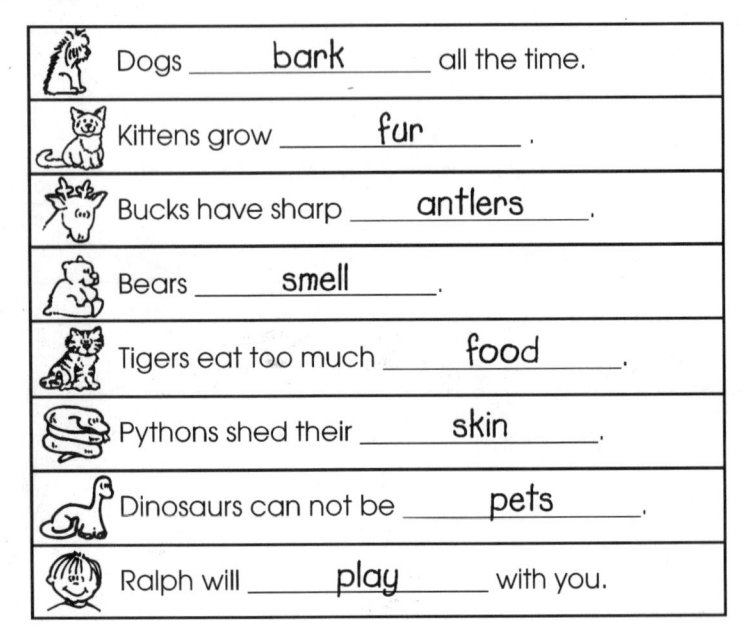

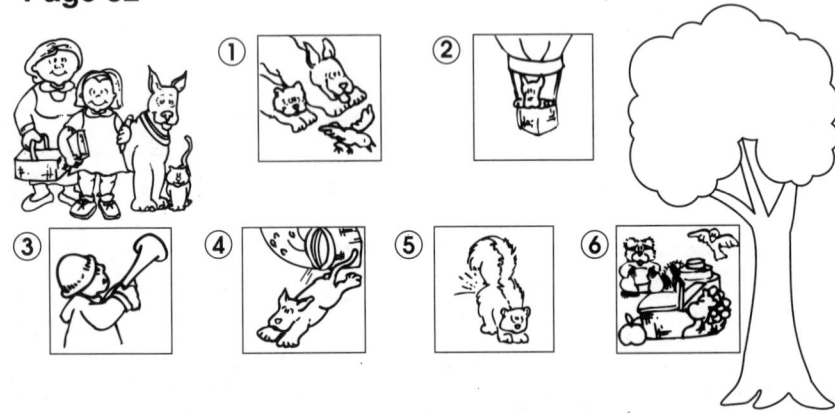

	Dogs ___bark___ all the time.	
	Kittens grow ___fur___.	
	Bucks have sharp ___antlers___.	
	Bears ___smell___.	
	Tigers eat too much ___food___.	
	Pythons shed their ___skin___.	
	Dinosaurs can not be ___pets___.	
	Ralph will ___play___ with you.	

Page 32

64